LET'S PLAY GAMES
IN CHINESE

TAO-CHUNG YAO
SCOTT MCGINNIS

Cheng & Tsui Company
Boston • Worcester

Let's Play Games in Chinese

Copyright © 2002 by Tao-chung Yao and Scott McGinnis

First Cheng & Tsui Revised Edition 2002

Published by

Cheng & Tsui Company
25 West Street
Boston, MA 02111-1213 USA
Fax (617) 426-3669
www.cheng-tsui.com
"Bringing Asia to the World"™

Library of Congress Control Number: 2002 141131

Illustrations: Tamara Visco

Quality Paperback ISBN 0-88727-360-2

10 9 8 7 6 5 4 3 2 1

Printed in the United States of America

Dedicated to our wives

Kuang-tien

and

Rebecca Grace

Acknowledgments

The authors thank the following for their assistance:

John D'Andrea
Vivian Hsu
Timothy Light
Ling-ling Liu
Craig Stevenson
Timothy C. Wong

CONTENTS

18. Card Games

FOREWORD

America's most conspicuous successes in foreign-language teaching have been at the beginning level and with those aspects of language that reflect relatively clear rule governing. In linguistic terms, we have been particularly adept at transmitting to our students the major surface-structure sentence types of the languages we have tried to teach. In teaching terms, we have been most efficient at pattern drill, both in grammar and in the sound system.

The result of our achievements has been that students who have completed a beginning course in most languages in the United States are notably quick and accurate in responding to a given set of very frequent linguistic cues. Our students excel in the *shapes* of the language. It is not at all uncommon for Americans on their first trip to an area where their target language is spoken to be complimented on their pronunciation and apparently easy fluency. At the more demanding tasks in a foreign language--negotiations, doing business, rapid translation, etc. (i.e., at tasks that require substantial *communicative proficiency* in the language)--we Americans are not generally accounted among the world's most able or well trained. Indeed native speakers of the languages we try to learn are often unhappily surprised to find that our superficial fluency in the rudiments of the language is not backed up by sufficient knowledge and facility to make real communication possible, and, more often than most of us would like to admit, conversations that begin in Chinese, Japanese, or French turn to English when the topic becomes important.

Nowhere is this more in evidence than among students of Chinese. It is almost a cliché now to hear Chinese teachers in China comment that the young Americans who come to China to continue their Chinese study are better than most in their *basic* oral skills when they first arrive. It is, unfortunately, just as common to hear that the long-term progress of those students is often not as rapid or as thorough as that of students from other nations. For it is in actual *use* of the language--rather than in responding mechanically to set classroom exercises--that we Americans fall down. Full grasp of the cultural implications of phrases that appear to be informational (but are not), acquaintance with the fast-speech rules of the language (which cause the speaker to elide over many of the consonants, vowels, and even tones that we listen to for cues), and the ability to control more than a few syllables between pauses--all these skills are vital to any post-beginning command of a language and are things at which most of us do not excel.

We have not demanded a level of foreign-language proficiency that calls for flexibility and subtlety in the languages we study. We have, instead, settled for rapid habitual responses to set phrases in set circumstances and nodding acquaintance with the real language demands beyond that rather elementary level. We have always assumed that our business and diplomacy (and friendships?) could be undertaken with the aid of interpreters if matters were of much importance.

Our language deficit has gotten us into increasing amounts of trouble over the past two decades. In addition to well known gaffes and our dangerous shortage of truly bilingual people in the foreign service and international business, we are told with increasing bluntness and increasing frequency by bilingual speakers from other countries that our deficiencies are indeed deficiencies and that it is our responsibility to repair them, rather than rely on the rest of the world to speak sophisticated English once the pleasantries are out of the way and serious matters begin.

There are many reasons for our deficits. Many steps will have to be taken to prepare text materials that will remedy our problems. Our field has been greatly aided in this effort by a nationwide interest in the "language proficiency" movement. Based on the successful experience of the State Department's Foreign Service Institute, the proficiency movement calls for the setting of specific performance goals for language classes and then measurement to see if those goals have been achieved. The performance goals are set in all four language skills (speaking, listening, reading, and writing) and can be stated (for Chinese) in roughly the following way:

Can the student book a hotel room in Beijing?

Can the student read street signs in a Chinese city?

Can the student understand replies to his or her requests for directions?

Can the student write an intelligible note to a friend about an appointment that must be missed?

The proficiency guidelines developed for all of the major languages taught in the United States contain hundreds of questions like these, ranged at different levels of attainment, so that the demands made of a beginning student will (naturally) be different from those of an advanced student and so that it will be clear what we mean by "beginning" and "advanced" in practical, operational terms. The ultimate goal of this movement is to enable us to begin training people who will attain a level where they can perform their jobs entirely in the target language. The fact that most serious business in government, the private sector, and in academia continues to be conducted in English is a measure of how far we have to go. But we have made some progress simply by identifying those skills and topics that are crucial to our use of a foreign language.

Real progress, of course, will come only when we have available for use teaching materials designed to help students develop those specific skills. A few of the more experienced teachers in the field are engaged in preparing such materials in book, tape, video, and computer formats, and the coming few years promise the appearance of several new, specifically targeted, and interesting teaching materials that will make learning and teaching Chinese easier and that will enable our students to reach ever higher standards of proficiency.

One of the first examples of such material is Yao and McGinnis's *Let's Play Games in Chinese*. This book is a most welcome addition to the language teacher's stock of tools. Among our language-learning deficits in American foreign-language teaching has been neglect of the need to have fun in the language we are learning, the need to interact with others, the need to engage in complex activities (that is, more complex than simple drills) that draw on our language and our mental skills in the same ways that most interactions in life do. This neglect is not universal in language teaching. In Britain and Europe, successful language teaching has long included much activity-based learning with games, songs, poetry and other recitation as a prominent and much loved part of the curriculum. In the British approach to teaching English as a foreign language, W.R. Lee's classic *Language-Teaching Games and Contests* must have provided helpful material for tens of thousands of teachers and millions of students over the past three decades. What Yao and McGinnis have done for Chinese teaching in this book is very similar to what Lee did for the teaching of English--that is, provide materials and inspiration for getting language out of the book, out of the tape recorder, and out of the stock memorized phrases and *into* real use in a setting that is *fun*.

That word *fun* does not enter our academic vocabulary much. You won't find it in most syllabi or textbooks--or in books on how to teach. And to be properly academic in writing this foreword I have written five pages before daring to use it. But we all know in our hearts that learning that we are interested in, enjoy, and that engages our whole attention is easy and successful learning, while learning that is a chore is just that, a *chore,* and is not nearly so successful. *Let's Play Games in Chinese* is one answer to the need for real enjoyment in learning. Yao and McGinnis are an ideal team to produce such a book and have brought to it a deep understanding of that simple (and frequently neglected) fact of human psychology. Tao-chung Yao's native language is Mandarin Chinese. He was educated through college in Taiwan before coming to the United States. Like his Chinese-language students, he is a second-language learner--a most successful one and a model for the rest of us. His scholarly articles in English are published in the most prestigious journals in the country. He has been teaching Chinese in the United States for a decade and a half, and in his teaching, he has developed materials in all media (video, computers, audiotape, and, of course, books). These have brought his classes alive, made them active and fun, and thereby raised the standard of proficiency of his students. The current book is the culmination of a decade of work on a set of games for Chinese-language students. The first examples were published in the *Journal of the Chinese Language Teachers Association.* They received such a positive response that expanding them and preparing a separately published book was clearly called for. Scott McGinnis, still a graduate student, is a native speaker of American

English. He began to study Chinese in the military, and continued in the intensive program at Cornell University and eventually for a year at the Beijing Language Institute in the People's Republic of China. For the past several years, he has been teaching first- and second-year Chinese to other Americans at Ohio State. Originally trained as an actor, he shares Yao's instinctive understanding of the need to make language learning active, engaged, and fun for it to be successful.

I envy the Chinese-language students and teachers who will use this book. When I began to study the language in 1965, our teacher had only one game in her repertoire and one song (*Sanzhi Laohu*--"Three Tigers"). That same teacher informed us on the first day of class that we foreigners would never learn to speak, write, or comprehend much of the language; all we could expect would be to decipher written texts with the aid of a dictionary. When I first began to teach Chinese in 1974, little more was available, and our goals were similarly constrained. Since then, however, quite a few Americans have been forced by circumstances to write letters and even articles, negotiate, attend lectures, and give speeches in Chinese. The demands now being made on us when we are in China are no different from those made on other foreigners--and no different from the demands that we place on the Chinese who come to the United States. We, too, must use the language and use it well enough to be well understood. These heightened expectations promise us a very exciting time, for finally Chinese classes are being held to standards similar to those held for French and Spanish classes. Increasingly, what goes on in our classes must resemble the best of what other languages are doing successfully. We will not meet these high expectations with the limited aspirations of two decades ago or with materials used a decade ago. But with active, enjoyable, and practical materials such as the games that Yao and McGinnis provide, we have a good chance of making a real start toward meeting those expectations. I envy those who have this book waiting for them in their beginning Chinese study!

Timothy Light
Kalamazoo College

PREFACE

Introduction

Why a book on Chinese language games? Or, for that matter, why a book on language games at all? The answer to the former can be answered somewhat simplistically by the fact that there has never been one in English. As for the latter query, other authors have demonstrated on paper and in practice the advisability of employing such activities for other languages. In our opinion, the time is quite ripe for such games in the Chinese classroom.

Yet the very word "game" is misleading, as it may suggest that the activity is nonconstructive, diversionary, or even downright frivolous. Nothing could be further from the truth for our purposes. We present here games that do not take away from learning time, but can in fact be part of the learning time. To be sure, the selection of content and the execution of these games is a delicate matter. Without proper care, they could well prove to be no more than idle pastimes.

Guidelines for Game Construction

Toward these ends, we have employed the following principles in the construction of games for learning Chinese. We have done our utmost to follow them, each of which we believe to be of no small importance.

(1) The game must aid the student in developing at least one of the four basic skills; namely, speaking, listening, reading, and writing.

(2) The game must also serve a clear purpose for a specific area of skill acquisition-- e.g., numbers, antonyms, the ba-pattern, etc.

(3) It should be possible to integrate the game into the regular classroom drill routine.

(4) The game should be playable on a variety of levels, most ideally from beginning through advanced.

(5) The game should ideally be cost-free, or at least low-cost.

(6) The game should be as simple as possible without being too childish. Overly elaborate schemes will only prove confusing, detracting from the ultimate goal of language acquisition. And while there are some fairly elaborate items within this collection, their complexity does not detract from the ultimate goal.

(7) Complementary to point 6, the game should ideally be one with which the American student is familiar. One will note that the inspiration for many of our exercises comes from a variety of popular games. This serves to further simplify their explanation to the students.

(8) The game should be designed so that in some form or another, every student is as actively involved as possible, thereby at least unconsciously consolidating his or her knowledge.

(9) The game should be playable within a reasonably short period of time (five to fifteen minutes).

(10) The game should be fun. Without this guideline, the situations described here would still be effective drills, but would lack the "punch" that makes them a delightful and enlightened vehicle for learning.

Suggestions for Use

While we have primarily (and understandably) designed our book with the Chinese language teacher in mind, there is no inherent reason to restrict use of these games to the Chinese language classroom. Their use at class parties or language camps seems very appropriate. In fact, many of them require no direct instructor supervision, as the level of complexity is basic enough (and the average student's competitive spirit is keen enough) that mistakes will be duly detected. For such games, the role of "instructor" indicated in the game instructions may well be served by a student.

Nevertheless, we take pains to point out that however "user-friendly" (where "user" = "student") these games may be, they are most effective when used under the supervision of a teacher who can take full advantage of the "lessons" they provide, as well as ensure that students are not developing erroneous language habits. Above all else, we emphasize the fact that these games cannot replace the actual teaching of language, but can indeed serve to improve it.

With this as preface, we provide the following more specific suggestions:

(1) Use these exercises for practice and review of concepts and patterns already learned. Do not use a game before or at the very start of learning the aspect of Chinese addressed or alluded to in the activity.

(2) Use the index or the special recommendations given for many of the games, so as to select those that complement the concepts being addressed at any given time in the course of study.

(3) Do not overuse any one game during a course.

(4) Do not use more than one game per class period, and that one for no more than ten to fifteen minutes. For language camps and parties, of course, a larger number of games may be employed effectively.

(5) Use the games selectively, particularly in response to those days when students need either a bit of "perking up" or a respite from the rigors of daily drill.

(6) To make maximum use of classroom time, an explanation of the game procedures, distributed to the students a day or two before the game, may be helpful. For several of the more complicated games involving student as well as instructor preparation, such details are provided for in the game description. The instructor can alternatively ask the students to read the game procedures directly from the book.

(7) Stay alert to student participation level. Each student must take part as prescribed in the game instructions for the activity to benefit all students at all times.

(8) Do not hesitate to praise the winners, including the awarding of prizes under appropriate conditions. By the same token, however, do not mete out any sort of punishment to losers. Remember, and remind your students, that the main purpose for these games, as for the course in toto, is to learn to use the Chinese language, not to win.

A Final Note

Perhaps the best thing that can be said about these games for learning Chinese is that they are an extremely entertaining way to use the language. It is the word "use" that is of paramount importance. There are numerous ways by which we can assess a student's ability to use the target language, be it memorized dialogues or written compositions. Yet these very means of purportedly promoting a student's progress in fact inhibits a portion of the student population. It is that portion that, intimidated by the pressures of a graded activity, may find the chance to freely practice without pressure, and to practice very well indeed, while playing these games.

Similarly, while the introduction of a competitive atmosphere is somewhat artificial, it is such an atmosphere that proves to be a better incentive than grades to certain students in helping bring out their best. We do not advocate a strict carrot-and-stick approach, in the form of prizes, for our fellow language teachers. But the greater the range of activities available, the more exciting and stimulating the classroom will be. One could not ask for more than that in any educational endeavor.

We offer *Let's Play Games in Chinese* in the spirit of the old expression pāozhuān-yǐnyù 抛砖引玉 , and hope that our audience may both profit by and take pleasure in the activities it contains. So, let the games begin!

1. POPULAR AMERICAN GAMES AND VARIANTS THEREOF

Simon Says

Body parts variation
Skills addressed: Listening, Speaking
Suggested level of usage: Elementary
Group size: 5-12
Equipment needed: None

Directions:
(1) The students stand up and gather around in a circle.

(2) The instructor says names of parts of the body (e.g., ěrduo 耳朵 [ear], bízi 鼻子 [nose]), either with or without a preceding Xīmén shuō 西門說(Simon says). If s/he says the catch phrase, students must point to that part of the body with their hand. If s/he does not, the students take no action. Any student who makes a mistake is to come to the front and play Xīmén 西門 (Simon).

(3) The student continues to be "Simon" until s/he catches another student making a mistake.

(4) Play continues until a designated time limit.

Action variation
Skills addressed: Listening, Speaking

Suggested level of usage: Elementary or intermediate
Group size: 5-12
Equipment needed: None

Directions:
(1) The students stand up and gather around in a circle.

(2) Either with or without the preface Xīmén shuō (Simon says), the instructor calls out actions that are known to and can be physically performed by the students -- e.g., xiào 笑 (laugh), kū 哭 (cry), pǎo 跑 (run). If the instructor says the aforementioned catch phrase, the students must perform the action stated. If s/he does not, the students remain immobile. Any student who makes a mistake is asked to play Xīmén.

(3) The student continues to be "Simon" until s/he catches another student making a mistake.

(4) Play continues until a designated time limit.

Bǎ-pattern variation

Skills addressed: Listening, Speaking
Suggested level of usage: Elementary
Group size: 5-12
Equipment needed: Standard classroom equipment and students' everyday belongings

Directions:
(1) The students stand up and gather around in a circle.

2

(2) The instructor utilizes the <u>bǎ</u> (把)-sentence pattern to issue a series of "orders"; e.g.,

<u>Xīmén shuō</u>: "Bǎ nǐmende shǒu fàng zài tóushang."
西門說： "把你們的手放在頭上."

<u>Xīmén shuō</u>: "Bǎ nǐmende shū dǎkai."
西門說： "把你們的書打開."

<u>Xīmén shuō</u>: "Bǎ nǐmende bǐ fàng zài kǒudàili."
西門說： "把你們的筆放在口袋裏."

Following each statement above, the students must put their hands on top of their heads, open their books, etc. However, when the instructor says a sentence not preceded by <u>Xīmén shuō</u> (e.g., <u>Bǎ shū náqilai</u> 把書拿起來), any student who does indeed pick up a book must come to the front and play Xīmén.

(3) The student continues to be "Simon" until s/he catches another student making a mistake.

(4) Play continues until a designated time limit.

Written variation
Skill addressed: Reading
Suggested level of usage: Elementary or higher
Group size: Flexible
Equipment needed: None

Directions:
(1) Before the game, the teacher writes out a number of commands on separate 8.5x11 sheets of paper. These commands can be simple verbs (<u>xiào</u> 笑, <u>pǎo</u> 跑), or might

employ the b<u>ă</u>-sentence pattern (e.g., <u>Bǎ nǐmende shū dǎkāi!</u> 把 你 們 的 書 打 開). Additionally, some of the commands should be preceded by <u>Xīmén shuō</u> 西門說 and others left plain.

(2) The teacher shows a sheet to the class. If the catch phrase <u>Xīmén shuō</u> 西門說 is included, the students must follow the instruction. If it is not, the students take no action. Any student who disobeys this latter dictum is out of the game.

(3) Play continues until all the sheets have been shown, or until a designated time limit.

Aural Bingo

Numbers variation
Skills addressed: Listening, Reading, Writing
Suggested level of usage: Elementary
Group size: Flexible
Equipment needed: Bingo cards (explained below), slips of paper (for instructor)

Directions:
(1) Before starting the game, the instructor writes each of the numbers one through ten on a separate slip of paper.

(2) The students are instructed to draw a nine-box square (3x3) and fill each box with one of the Chinese characters for the numbers one through ten. The numbers may be arranged in any order, but a number may not be repeated.

(3) The class chooses a pattern (e.g., T, L, H, X) that will be used for the game.

(4) The instructor draws the character-inscribed slips of paper one at a time and reads it aloud (in Chinese) to the students. If a student has written that character on his/her card, s/he circles or otherwise marks the card.

(5) The first person who completes the selected pattern shouts bīnguǒ 賓果 (bingo). If s/he has made no mistakes, s/he is the winner.

(6) The game may be repeated as often as time permits, with new cards drawn each time, and new patterns frequently utilized to add variety.

5

(7) Additionally, the complexity of the numbers may be increased as the students' vocabulary expands. When utilizing multi-digit numbers, the instructor can write a list of Arabic numerals on the blackboard and require the students to write them in character form on their cards. Otherwise, the rules are unchanged.

Homophone variation

Skills addressed: Listening, Reading, Writing
Suggested level of usage: Advanced
Group size: Flexible
Equipment needed: Bingo cards (explained below), slips of paper, blackboard, chalk

Directions:

(1) Before the game, the instructor compiles a nine-character list of homophones and writes each character on a separate slip of paper.

(2) The instructor then writes this list of characters on the blackboard.

(3) The students are instructed to draw their 3x3 bīnguǒ 賓果 (bingo) squares and fill the squares with the characters in random order.

(4) The students select a pattern for the game (e.g., L, T, X, H).

(5) The instructor draws the character-inscribed slips one at a time and reads it aloud in a polysyllabic compound the students know. For example, if the homophone is shì the

instructor's examples may include <u>shìjiè</u> 世界, <u>shìqing</u> 事情, etc.

(6) The first student who completes the selected pattern shouts <u>bīnguǒ</u> 賓果 (bingo). If s/he has made no mistakes, s/he is the winner.

(7) This game may be repeated as often as time permits, with new patterns utilized to add variety.

(8) A further variation of this game might be to use words that are not strictly homophones but that differ only in tone (e.g., <u>bǎo</u> 保, <u>bào</u> 報, <u>bāo</u> 包), or whose closely related pronunciation causes them to be easily confused (e.g., <u>qù</u> 去/<u>chū</u> 出, <u>xú</u> 徐 /<u>shū</u> 書). This variation could even be used by beginning and intermediate students.

Mutual radical variation

Skills addressed:	Listening, Reading, Writing
Suggested level of usage:	Advanced
Group size:	Flexible
Equipment needed:	Bingo cards (explained below), slips of paper, blackboard, chalk

Directions:
(1) Before the game, the instructor selects 9, 16, or 25 characters with the same radical that the students have learned and writes each on a separate slip of paper.

(2) The instructor writes the list of characters on the blackboard.

7

(3) The students are instructed to draw a 3x3, 4x4, or 5x5 bīnguǒ 賓果 (bingo) square and fill it with the characters in random order.

(4) The students select a pattern for the game (e.g., H, L, T, X).

(5) The instructor draws the character-inscribed slips one at a time and reads it aloud to the students. For homophones, the instructor reads the word in a polysyllabic compound the students know.

(6) The first student who completes the selected pattern shouts bīnguǒ 賓果 (bingo). If s/he has made no mistakes, s/he is the winner.

(7) Again, patterns may be changed from round to round to add variety to the game.

Compound words variation

Skills addressed: Listening, Reading, Writing
Suggested level of usage: Elementary or higher
Group size: Flexible
Equipment needed: Paper, pen, blackboard, chalk

Directions:
(1) Before the game the instructor selects at least nine (or alternatively, 16 or 25) compound words of a unified semantic class. Such classes may include time words, clothing, food and drink, household items, etc. The instructor writes each word on a separate slip of paper.

8

(2) The instructor writes this list of compound words on the blackboard before class begins.

(3) The students are instructed to draw their 3x3 (or 4x4 or 5x5) game cards, filling each square with one compound from the list on the blackboard.

(4) The students select a game pattern (e.g., L, T, H, X).

(5) The instructor draws the character-inscribed slips one at a time and reads them aloud. If a student has written that character on his/her card, s/he circles or otherwise marks the card.

(6) The first person who completes the selected pattern shouts <u>bīnguǒ</u> 賓果(bingo). If s/he has made no mistakes, s/he is the winner.

9

Visual Bingo

Measure words variation
Skills addressed: Reading, Writing
Suggested level of usage: Elementary or higher
Group size: Flexible
Equipment needed: Paper, blackboard, chalk, visuals (explained below)

Directions:

(1) Before the game, the instructor selects at least nine measure words the students know and writes them on the blackboard.

(2) The students are instructed to draw their bīnguǒ 賓果 (bingo) cards and fill the squares with the measure words in random order.

(3) The students select a game pattern (e.g., L, T, H, X).

(4) The instructor shows the students nominals that match the measure words. The nominals may be shown in a variety of ways. The instructor may exhibit the actual object (e.g., books, pens, paper, etc.), display cards with the words written on them, or write the words on the blackboard. Whatever method is used, the students then mark on their cards the measure words that match the nominal.

(5) The first student who completes the pattern shouts bīnguǒ 賓果 (bingo). If s/he has made no mistakes, s/he is the winner.

10

Antonym variation
               Skills addressed: Reading, Writing
     Suggested level of usage: Elementary or higher
                   Group size: Flexible
         Equipment needed: Paper, pens, blackboard, chalk

Directions:

(1) Before the game, the instructor selects at least nine pairs of antonyms, writing one half of each pair on the chalkboard, and the other halves on separate sheets of paper.

(2) The students draw their 3x3 game cards and fill the bīnguǒ 賓果 (bingo) squares with characters from the list on the board in random order.

(3) The students select a game pattern (e.g., L, T, H, X).

(4) The instructor selects one character at a time from the set of sheets and shows it to the students. The students are to find the antonym shown on their game cards.

(5) The first student who completes the selected pattern shouts bīnguǒ 賓果 (bingo). If s/he has made no mistakes, s/he is the winner.

Simplified/complex form variation
               Skills addressed: Reading, Writing
     Suggested level of usage: Elementary or higher
                   Group size: Flexible
         Equipment needed: Paper, pens, blackboard, chalk

Directions:

(1) Before the game, the instructor selects 9 (or alternatively, 16 or 25) characters the students have learned, writing the simplified (or complex) forms each on a separate sheet of paper, and the complex (or simplified) versions on the blackboard.

(2) The students draw their 3x3 (or 4x4 or 5x5) game cards, filling each square with one character from the list on the blackboard.

(3) The students select a game pattern (e.g., L, T, H, X).

(4) The instructor displays one sheet of paper at a time. The students find the equivalent complex (or simplified) form on their game cards.

(5) The first student who completes the selected pattern shouts <u>bīnguǒ</u> 賓果 (bingo). If s/he has made no mistakes, s/he is the winner.

Twenty Questions

Numbers variation

Skills addressed: Speaking, Listening
Suggested level of usage: Elementary
Group size: 5-20
Equipment needed: None

Directions:

(1) The instructor (or the class) determines the range within which the number to be guessed is to be drawn; e.g., from zero to 1000. Naturally, the range should complement the students' vocabulary range.

(2) The instructor (or a student) selects a student to be "it," and a number for that student to guess. The student has a twenty-question limit within which to determine that number. The "it" can ask any of his/her classmates, preferably jumping around to give everybody a chance to speak. When answering a question, the student must give a full sentence, not just a word.

(3) Particularly for the first-year students, this is an excellent opportunity to practice their mastery of numerals, the use of bǐ 比 (compare) and choice-type questions using háishì 還 是 (or). Below is an example sequence for a round of this version of twenty questions. The number being guessed is 786.

Zhèige shùmù bǐ wǔbǎi dà háishì bǐ wǔbǎi xiǎo?
這個數目比五百大還是比五百小？

<u>Zhèige shùmù bǐ qībǎi wǔshí dà háishì bǐ qībǎi wǔshí xiǎo?</u>
這個數目比七百五十大還是比七百五十小?

<u>Zhèige shùmù bǐ bābǎi dà háishì bǐ bābǎi xiǎo?</u>
這個數目比八百大還是比八百小?

<u>Zhèige shùmù bǐ qībǎi qīshí wǔ dà háishì bǐ qībǎi qīshí wǔ xiǎo?</u>
這個數目比七百七十五大還是比七百七十五小?

<u>Zhèige shùmù bǐ qībǎi bāshí dà háishì bǐ qībǎi bāshí xiǎo?</u>
這個數目比七百八十大還是比七百八十小?

<u>Zhèige shùmù bǐ qībǎi jiǔshí dà háishì bǐ qībǎi jiǔshí xiǎo?</u>
這個數目比七百九十大還是比七百九十小?

<u>Zhèige shùmù bǐ qībǎi bāshí wǔ dà háishì bǐ qībǎi bāshí wǔ xiǎo?</u>
這個數目比七百八十五大還是比七百八十五小?

<u>Zhèige shùmù shìbushì qībǎi bāshí liù?</u>
這個數目是不是七百八十六?

Object location variation
Skills addressed: Speaking, Listening
Suggested level of usage: Elementary
Group size: 5-20
Equipment needed: Wristwatch, students' everyday belongings (e.g., books, notebooks, backpacks)

Directions:

(1) A student is selected to be "it" and leaves the room.

(2) While s/he is out of the room, the wristwatch is hidden somewhere out of plain sight (e.g., in a student's book).

(3) The student who is "it" returns to the center of the room. S/he is allowed a total of twenty questions through which s/he attempts to ascertain the location of the watch. The student can ask any of his/her classmates, but the questions must be asked in grammatically correct Chinese. Additionally, these questions must be of a choice-type format (as opposed to one employing a straight question word--e.g., <u>Biǎo zài shénme dìfang</u> 錶 在 什 麼 地 方?). As a means for other students to practice speaking, it is essential to make a rule that, when answering questions, the players must give full sentences, not just words, as answers.

(4) Here is an example sequence of questions suitable for an elementary-level class:

<u>Biǎo zài wǒde qiántou háishì zài wǒde hòutou?</u>
錶在我的前頭還是在我的後頭?

<u>Biǎo zài wǒde zuǒbiān háishì zài wǒde yòubiān?</u>
錶在我的左邊還是在我的右邊?

Now that the general vicinity has been narrowed down (say to the front and left of "it"), the student may ask questions such as:

Biǎo shìbushì zài rénshēnshang?
錶是不是在人身上?

Biǎo shìbushì zài zhuōzishang?
錶是不是在桌子上?

If the student has now ascertained the watch to be on a table, upon which numerous items may be piled, s/he may wish to ask:

Biǎo shìbushì zài shūbāoli?
錶是不是在書包裏?

Biǎo shìbushì zài běnzi xiàtou?
錶是不是在本子下頭?

Supposing that this last question yields a positive answer, the "it" student can now ask individually of the classmates to the left and front of him/her:

Biǎo shìbushì zài nǐde běnzi xiàtou?
錶是不是在你的本子下頭?

Provided there are fewer than 15 students in that direction, and each student has no more than one book on his/her desk, the designated "it" should succeed in finding the watch.

(5) When the student has found the object, s/he designates a new player to be "it," and the entire game sequence commences once again.

Object identification variation
Skills addressed: Speaking, Listening
Suggested level of usage: Elementary or higher
Group size: 5-20
Equipment needed: Standard classroom equipment
(e.g., chairs, desks)

Directions:
(1) One student is selected to be "it," and another student selects an object within sight to be the subject of the questions.

(2) The student has a twenty-question limit within which to determine the object. The student can ask any of his/her classmates, preferably jumping around to give everybody a chance. When answering a question, the student must give a full sentence, not just a word.

(3) The range of queries in this game is limited only by the students' proficiency. Any question save that of asking directly (to wit, Zhèige dōngxi shì shénme 這個東西是什麼?) is permissible. For example, the following sequence might be observed in a beginning or intermediate-level classroom:

Q: Zhèige dōngxi zài wǒde qiántou háishì zài wǒde hòutou?
這個東西在我的前頭還是在我的後頭?

A: Nèige dōngxi zài nǐde qiántou.
那個東西在你的前頭。

17

Q: Zhèige dōngxi bǐ shū dà háishì bǐ shū xiǎo?
這個東西比書大還是比書小？

A: Nèige dōngxi bǐ shū dà.
那個東西比書大。

Q: Zhèige dōngxi yǒu méiyǒu yánsè?
這個東西有沒有顏色？

A: Nèige dōngxi yǒu yánsè.
那個東西有顏色。

Q: Zhèige dōngxi shìbushì báide?
這個東西是不是白的？

A: Nèige dōngxi búshì báide.
那個東西不是白的。

Q: Zhèige dōngxi shì chángde háishì duǎnde?
這個東西是長的還是短的？

A: Nèige dōngxi bùcháng yě bùduǎn.
那個東西不長也不短。

Q: Zhèige dōngxi shì fāngde háishì yuánde?
這個東西是方的還是圓的？

A: Nèige dōngxi shì fāngde.
那個東西是方的。

Q: <u>Zhèige dōngxi shìbushì yòng zhǐ zuòde?</u>
這個東西是不是用紙做的?

A: <u>Nèige dōngxi búshì yòng zhǐ zuòde.</u>
那個東西不是用紙做的。

Q: <u>Zhèige dōngxi shìbushì yòng mùtou zuòde?</u>
這個東西是不是用木頭做的?

A: <u>Nèige dōngxi shì yòng mùtou zuòde.</u>
那個東西是用木頭做的。

From the above series of questions, the student should be close to identifying the object in question as a chair to the front of him/her.

(4) For more advanced students, the "object" selected may be more complex, such as a physical movement (walking, running, driving a car), or even an abstract concept (e.g., happiness, democracy, war).

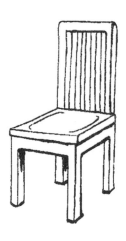

Musical Chairs

Skills addressed: Reading, Speaking
Suggested level of usage: Elementary or higher
Group size: 8-10
Equipment needed: Chairs, paper, magic markers, tape recorder.

Directions:

(1) The teacher copies down 40 to 50 characters from the lesson(s) the class has learned, one character per sheet.

(2) The teacher asks the students to move their chairs into a circle. There should be the same number of chairs as students.

(3) The teacher then puts the character sheets face down on the chairs, one per chair, so that no one can see what's written on the paper.

(4) The teacher asks each student to stand in front of one of the chairs.

(5) The teacher then turns on the music, and the students start to move clockwise around the chairs. After a few seconds, the teacher turns off the music and the students stop.

(6) Each student is to pick up the character sheet on the chair right beside him/her and read the character aloud. While pronouncing the character, s/he should hold the sheet up so everybody can see it. If the student pronounces

the character correctly, s/he keeps the sheet; if not, s/he puts it back on the chair.

(7) The teacher then fills up the empty chairs with other character sheets and the game continues.

(8) When the teacher has used up all the character sheets, there will be empty chairs with no character sheets on them. This is perfectly all right, as those who happen to stop by the empty chairs simply do not get a chance to earn a sheet.

(9) The game ends when all the sheets have been taken by the students or when the predetermined time is up. The student who gets the most sheets is the winner.

The Buzz Game

Skills addressed: Listening, Speaking
Suggested level of usage: Elementary
Group size: Flexible
Equipment needed: None

Directions:

(1) The students form a circle.

(2) Using Chinese, the students count off in sequence, one number per student. If the student's number is either a multiple of seven (including 7 itself) or has 7 in it, s/he must clap his/her hands instead of saying the number. If s/he does say the number--or, if during the course of "counting off," s/he says any number incorrectly--s/he loses one point.

(3) Play continues until a designated time limit or to a predetermined number (e.g., 100 or 1000). The student who loses the fewest points is the winner.

2. TELEVISION GAME SHOWS AND VARIANTS THEREOF

Class Feud

Oral variation

Skills addressed: Listening, Speaking
Suggested level of usage: Elementary or higher
Group size: Flexible
Equipment needed: None

Directions:

(1) The teacher divides the class into two teams. Each team elects a leader.

(2) The teacher will ask the class to name things the class has learned by asking questions such as:

Name five different kinds of <u>bǐ</u> 筆 (writing instruments).
What are the colors that you can see in this room?
What are the four seasons of a year?

Teachers are encouraged to ask questions in Chinese if the questions are not beyond the students' level of proficiency.

(3) The leader of each team decides whether his/her team wants to play the round for each question asked. The leader who raises his/her hand first wins the right to play first for his/her team.

(4) The players of the playing team take turns naming one thing at a time in response to the given question. If a member of the team fails to come up with anything or says an incorrect word, that team loses its turn and the other team takes over and continues the game. For example, team A, having said qiānbǐ 鉛筆, gāngbǐ 鋼筆, and yuánzibǐ 原子筆, runs out of vocabulary and thus fails to complete naming five kinds of bǐ 筆. The teacher, after five seconds of waiting, announces that it is now team B's turn. Team B could continue and win the round by saying fěnbǐ 粉筆 and máobǐ 毛筆. However, if team B's first player said fěnbǐ 粉筆 but the second player failed to say anything in the next five seconds, the turn goes back to team A's player who is next in line. The team that completes answering a question, even if it did not start answering the question, will be the winner of that round.

(5) If none of the teams wish to answer a certain question, the teacher should provide the class with the correct answer and ask the students to review the words.

(6) The game ends when all the questions have been asked. The team that completes answering the most questions is the winner.

Written variation
     Skills addressed: Reading, Writing
     Suggested level of usage: Elementary or higher
     Group size: Flexible
     Equipment needed: Blackboard and chalk

24

Directions:

(1) The teacher divides the class into two teams. Each team elects a leader.

(2) The teacher asks the class to write down words the class has learned by asking questions such as:

> Write the names of five different kinds of bǐ 筆 (writing instruments).
> Write down the colors that you can see in this room.
> Write the Chinese words for the four seasons of a year.

Teachers are encouraged to ask questions in Chinese if the questions are not beyond the students' level of proficiency.

(3) The leader of each team decides whether his/her team wants to play the round for each question asked. The leader who raises his/her hand first wins the right to play first for his/her team.

(4) The players of the playing team take turns writing one item at a time in response to the given question. If a member of the team fails to write anything or writes a word incorrectly, that team loses its turn and the other team takes over and continues the game. For example, team A, having written qiānbǐ 鉛筆, gāngbǐ 鋼筆, and yuánzibǐ 原子筆 on the blackboard, runs out of vocabulary and thus fails to complete naming five kinds of bǐ 筆. The teacher, after five seconds of waiting, announces that it is now team B's turn. Team B could continue and win the round by writing fěnbǐ 粉筆 and máobǐ 毛筆. However, if team B's first player wrote fěnbǐ 粉筆, but the second player failed to write anything in the next five seconds,

25

the turn goes back to team A's player who is next in line. The team that completes answering a question, even if it did not start answering the question, will be the winner of that round.

(5) If none of the teams wish to answer a certain question, the teacher should provide the class with the correct answer and ask the students to review the words.

(6) The game ends when all the questions have been asked. The team that completes answering the most questions is the winner.

The Password Game

Skills addressed: Listening, Speaking, Reading
Suggested level of usage: Elementary or higher
Group size: Flexible
Equipment needed: Blackboard and chalk or paper and pencil

Directions:

(1) The instructor divides the class into two groups and asks each group to send one representative to the front of the classroom. The two representatives sit with their backs to the blackboard, facing the other students.

(2) The teacher flips a coin to decide which team starts the game. The teacher then chooses an expression the students have learned and either writes it on the blackboard or writes it on a piece of paper and shows it to everyone except the two team representatives.

(3) The students on the first team take turns giving their representative verbal clues to help him/her guess which expression was shown by the teacher. If after three guesses the representative still cannot guess the word, then the other team takes over and their representative also has three guessess. If the representative of the second team also fails, then the turn goes back to the first team.

(4) The students can use almost any clues they like, from one word to several sentences. The only restriction is that they cannot use any of the characters in the expression in question, or any gestures that explicitly indicate the object in question. For example, if the teacher gives the

27

expression shǒubiǎo 手錶 (wristwatch), the clues should contain neither shǒu 手 (hand) nor biǎo 錶 (watch), nor an explicit indication of or gesture pointing to a wristwatch. Violation of this rule will cause the team to lose its turn and the other team to take over.

(5) After a team correctly guesses the expression in question, it can continue to play until it loses its turn. Team representatives should rotate after each expression is guessed, so that all students have a chance to play.

(6) The game ends when the time is up or when all the expressions have been used. The team that has guessed the most expressions is the winning team.

3. SIMPLE VOCABULARY GAMES

Telling the Tones

Skill addressed: Listening
Suggested level of usage: Elementary or higher
Group size: Flexible
Equipment needed: None

Directions:

(1) The teacher prepares a list of expressions of one or two characters in length. They need not be expressions the students have learned.

(2) The teacher asks the students to use their fingers to show the tone they hear. One finger means the first tone; two fingers, the second tone, etc. To show neutral tone, the student simply makes a fist. For two-syllable words, one hand stands for each syllable.

(3) The teacher starts the game by reading an expression from the list and asking the students to tell the tone(s) by using their hands. If a student fails to get the tone(s) right, s/he loses one point.

(4) The game ends when all the expressions have been read. The student who has lost the fewest points is the winner.

(5) If the size of the class is too large (for example, 30 students), the teacher might find it hard to tell who has

given the right answer and who has not. One solution to this problem is to let the students keep a record of their own scores. An additional alternative is for students to form pairs facing each other, with each pair member keeping his/her opponent's score. At the end of the game, the teacher asks who lost the fewest points, thereupon declaring the winner.

Passing the Message

Oral variation

Skills addressed: Listening, Speaking
Suggested level of usage: Elementary or higher
Group size: Flexible (5-10 will be ideal)
Equipment needed: None

Directions:

(1) The teacher selects a sentence (at the students' proficiency level) and whispers it into the ear of the first player, making sure that no other player can hear it.

(2) The first player then whispers the sentence s/he heard to the second player, and so on.

(3) After hearing the sentence, the last player says it aloud so that everyone can hear it. The teacher then says the original sentence aloud.

(4) The fun part of this game is that, after passing through several mouths, the last sentence is often quite different from the original one.

Written variation

Skills addressed: Reading, Writing
Suggested level of usage: Elementary or higher
Group size: Flexible
Equipment needed: Paper and pencil

Directions:

(1) The teacher selects a sentence, writes it down on a piece of paper and shows it to the first student. The player is allowed to look at the sentence for 5 or 10 seconds. Then s/he writes the sentence down on his/her own piece of paper and shows it to the next student.

(2) Each student in turn follows the same procedure of looking at, writing down, and sharing the sentence.

(3) The last student, after seeing the sentence, writes it on the blackboard. The teacher also writes the original sentence on the blackboard.

(4) The sentence that the final student writes is often quite different from the original one. The teacher might want to ask all participating students to copy their sentences from their paper onto the blackboard and discuss with the students why or how mistakes were made. The teacher should also use this opportunity to point out the easily made mistakes so that the students can avoid them in the future.

4. AURAL/ORAL VOCABULARY GAMES

Merry-Go-Round

Syllable component variation
Skills addressed: Speaking, Listening
Suggested level of usage: Elementary or higher
Group size: 3-15
Equipment needed: None

Directions:

(1) The students and instructor sit in a circle, if conditions permit.

(2) The instructor commences play by saying a monosyllabic word (e.g., zǎo 早 [Good morning!], shū 書 [book]).

(3) The student sitting beside the instructor, or the first designated player, selects either the initial or final component of the instructor's word and uses it to form a new one. For instance, if the instructor's syllable was bào 報 (newspaper), the student may use either b or ao to make a different word (e.g., bā 八 [eight], gāo 高 [tall]). The tone does not need to be the same. In addition, the student must provide the English equivalent for his/her new word.

(4) If the student is able to create a new word and provides the proper meaning and correct pronunciation, s/he receives one point. However, if, for example, the student

33

says <u>hào</u> (with fourth tone) with a meaning of "good" (<u>hǎo</u> 好), s/he loses one point, and play rotates to the next student after the instructor corrects the mistake.

(5) Play continues until a designated time limit.

(6) For more advanced students, the syllable-formation rules may be made even stricter. A word may be divided up into its segmental and suprasegmental components (that is, the initial, final, and tone). The student will be required to retain two out of these three elements of his predecessor's word in creating his/her new one. For instance, if the teacher commences play with <u>lái</u> 來 (come), the student may keep the tone and the final (as in <u>bái</u> 白 [white]), or the initial and the tone (as in <u>lán</u> 藍 [blue]). As with the original formulation of the game, an English equivalent for the new word must be provided by the student, as well as the proper pronunciation, in order for him/her to stay in the game.

Full syllable variation
Skills addressed: Speaking, Listening
Suggested level of usage: Elementary or higher
Group size: 3-15
Equipment needed: None

Directions:
(1) The students and instructor sit in a circle, if conditions permit.

34

(2) The instructor starts the game by saying an expression of two or three syllables (e.g., <u>Yīngguóhuà</u> 英 國 話 [English], <u>xiězì</u> 寫字 [write characters]).

(3) The student sitting beside the instructor, or the first designated player, selects one syllable from the teacher's term and uses it to create a new expression. For instance, if the instructor's phrase was <u>xiězì</u> 寫字 (write characters), the first student may use either <u>xiě</u> or <u>zì</u> to form a different expression (e.g., <u>xiěxìn</u> 寫 信 [write letters], <u>Hànzì</u> 漢 字 [Chinese characters]). Ideally, the same lexical terms should be utilized. However, in the interest of a smoothly progressing game, homophones will be permitted. For example, if one player's expression was <u>shuōhuà</u> 說 話 (speak), the next player may use <u>huà</u> 畫 (painting) as well as <u>huà</u> 話 (word) to form his/her phrase.

(4) If the student is unable to keep the "merry-go-round" moving, s/he loses a point, and play rotates to the next student.

(5) Play continues until a fixed time limit.

Guessing the Words

Skills addressed: Reading, Writing, Speaking
Suggested level of usage: Elementary or higher
Group size: Flexible
Equipment needed: 3x5 cards, pens

Directions:

(1) Before the game, the teacher prepares a list of recently studied single and/or multiple-character words.

(2) Each student pairs up with a classmate.

(3) The teacher reads off the list of words. Each student copies the list on the 3x5 cards, one word per card.

(4) The students thereupon take turns guessing the words on each other's cards. Three points are given for correct first guess, two points for a correct second guess, and one point for a correct third guess. No points are given for a word not guessed in three tries, or if a student mispronounces the character in question, even if s/he does guess correctly.

(5) Students keep their own point totals. The student with the higher point total in each pair is the winner.

The Ball Game

Skills addressed: Speaking, Reading
Suggested level of usage: Elementary and higher
Group size: Flexible (for beginning
Chinese students, 10 players)
Equipment needed: Some white paper (8.5 x 11 will
be perfect), magic markers

Directions:

(1) The instructor assigns one number to each student and asks the student to write the number in Chinese on a piece of white paper. For students who have not yet learned how to write numbers in Chinese, Arabic numerals can be used. If there are ten elementary-level Chinese students playing this game, it is advised that they use the numbers 1 through 10. For more advanced students, higher numbers such as 74, 109, 258, etc. can be used. The numbers need not be consecutive for such a group.

(2) The students form a circle, each holding the number in front of him/herself so that all players can see it. The numbers need not be in any particular order.

(3) The player with the smallest number starts the game by saying:

Wǒde X (the player's number) qiú pèng Y (another player's number) qiú.
我的 X 球碰 Y 球。

The player whose number is called should respond immediately (say, within five seconds) by saying the same line, with the variation:

Wǒde Y qiú pèng Z (another person's number) qiú.
我的 Y 球碰 Z 球。

Play continues to rotate around the circle with the same pattern.

(4) If a player fails to realize that his/her number is being called, and thus fails to respond, or if a player makes a mistake by saying a number that is not represented by anyone (e.g., with eight players showing numbers 1 to 8, 9 or 10 will not be acceptable), or saying a number incorrectly (for example, wù instead of wǔ for 5), that player will be asked to step out of the circle or to put the paper behind him/her, to show that s/he is out of the game. The game then resumes with the student who said the last correct sentence.

(5) The game ends when a predetermined time is up or when there are only four or five students left. The players who are still "alive" at the end of the game will be the winners.

(6) One way to make this game more exciting is to ask the students to switch their papers several times during the game (for example, once every two minutes). This will force the players to know how to say more words correctly.

(7) To add competitive spirit, the teacher might want to split the class into two teams (for example, the odd-

number team and the even-number team). When two teams are playing against each other, players should try to "hit" the members of the other teams by calling the opponents' numbers rather than one's own team's numbers. The game ends when one of the two teams is completely wiped out, or when a predetermined time is up. In the latter case, the winning team will be the one with more survivors.

(8) For more advanced students, or for a larger class, the teacher might want to divide the class into 3 or 4 groups by assigning a different color to each team. The color can be represented by writing the numbers in magic markers of different colors. With the addition of a color distinction, the sentence being said should be

<u>Wǒde</u> (color of own team) (one's own number) <u>pèng</u> (color of another team) (number of another person).

Example: <u>Wǒde hóng wǔ pèng lán liù.</u>
我的紅五碰藍六。

(9) A final advanced variation of the game uses recently learned vocabulary items rather than numbers. For example, when learning clothing items, a student representing "hat" says:

<u>Wǒde màozi pèng xiézi.</u>
我的帽子碰鞋子。

The student representing "shoes" must immediately respond by saying something such as:

<u>Wǒde xiézi pèng kùzi.</u>
我的鞋子碰褲子。

(10) As a means to better train the students' ears, the teacher can put together some words that bear a resemblance in sound. For example:

<u>Shíjiān</u> 時間 (time), <u>shìjiè</u> 世界 (world), <u>shíxiàn</u> 實現 (to realize), <u>shíyàn</u> 實驗 (to experiment), <u>shíyóu</u> 石油 (petroleum), <u>shíyuè</u> 十月 (October), <u>shíjiàn</u> 實踐 (to carry out), etc.

40

Finding the Objects

Skills addressed: Listening, Speaking
Suggested level of usage: Elementary or higher
Group size: Flexible
Equipment needed: Various objects (corresponding to vocabulary students have learned), table

Directions:
(1) The teacher places all of the objects in plain view on the table.

(2) The teacher calls on one student at a time, telling him/her

Qǐng nǐ bǎ (name of item) gěi wǒ.
請你把 (name of item) 給我。

If the object is there, the student picks it up and gives it to the teacher, saying

Wǒ bǎ (name of item) gěi nǐ.
我把 (name of item) 給你。

If there is no such item on the tabletop, the student responds

41

<u>Duìbuqǐ! Wǒ bùnéng bǎ</u> (name of item) <u>gěi nǐ, yīnwei</u> <u>zhuōzishang méiyǒu</u> (name of item).

對不起! 我不能把 (name or item) 給你, 因爲桌子上沒有 (name of item)。

(3) Students are awarded one point for each item correctly identified and presented, and penalized one point for any mistakes in either object identification or pronunciation. The student with the highest point total at the end of the predetermined time period is the winner.

Do You Know What You Are?

Skills addressed: Speaking, Listening, Writing, Reading
Suggested level of usage: Elementary or higher
Group size: Flexible
Equipment needed: Blackboard, chalk, 8.5x11 paper, pens, straight pins

Directions:

(1) The teacher writes from five to ten recently learned vocabulary items on the blackboard. Each student chooses one and writes it on his/her 8.5x11 sheet of paper.

(2) After collecting the sheets, the teacher asks the students to line up with their backs toward him/her. The teacher then pins one sheet (different from the one the student wrote) on the back of each student.

(3) The students move about the room attempting to ascertain "what they are"-- i.e., what vocabulary item is pinned to their back. They may ask any other student any question in that process except a direct <u>Wǒ shì shénme</u> 我是什麼?

(4) When a student thinks s/he know what s/he is, s/he asks the teacher for confirmation. The first student to figure out what s/he is, is the winner.

43

Fill In the Names of the Places

Skill addressed: Listening
Suggested level of usage: Elementary
Group size: Flexible
Equipment needed: Handouts (explained below), pens

Directions:

(1) The teacher prepares a map with several streets and buildings, labeling some of the buildings (e.g., fànguǎn 飯館, shāngdiàn 商店) and leaving others blank.

(2) The teacher distributes this partially completed map to the students. Referring to a "master" on which all of the buildings are labeled, the teacher provides information by which the students can fill in their map. For example:

Fànguǎn gēn shāngdiànde zhōngjiān yǒu yíge jiàotáng.Jiàotáng zài xuéxiàode hòutou.
飯館跟商店的中間有一個教堂。教堂在學校的後頭。

(3) The teacher can either grade the student-filled-in maps outside of class or discuss the proper completion with the students in class.

(4) The student who did the best job of completing the map is the winner.

Name the Dishes

Skills addressed: Listening, Speaking
Suggested level of usage: Elementary or higher
Group size: Flexible
Equipment needed: Pictures of Chinese (food) dishes

Directions:

(1) The teacher prepares ten to twenty pictures of Chinese dishes. The easiest way to do this is to cut out some pictures from a Chinese cookbook. However, teachers with artistic talent can always draw the pictures themselves.

(2) Before playing the game, the teacher should teach the students how to say the names of the dishes, and also allow them some time to memorize the names.

(3) The teacher assigns a number to each of the students and writes the numbers down on paper, one per sheet. The teacher divides the students into two teams--the odd-number team and the even-number team. S/he also divides the number sheets into two piles--the odd-number pile and the even-number pile.

(4) The teacher pulls out one picture, shows it to the students, and asks one of the following questions:

Zhèige càide míngzi jiào shénme?
這個菜的名字叫什麼?

45

Zhèige cài jiào shénme?
這個菜叫什麼?

Zhèi shì shénme cài?
這是什麼菜?

(5) The teacher then draws a number from the odd-number pile. The student whose number is drawn must answer the question within three seconds. The sentence pattern the student uses must be the same as the one used by the teacher. If the student answers the question quickly and correctly, s/he earns two points for her/his team. If s/he fails to answer the question, one of her/his teammates can answer it, but will only receive one point if the answer is correct. If the second try also fails, the turn goes to the other team.

(6) The game ends when all the pictures have been shown or when the predetermined time is up. The team with the highest point total wins.

5. READING VOCABULARY GAMES

Call the Names First

Skills addressed: Reading, Speaking, Writing
Suggested level of usage: Elementary or higher
Group size: 5-10
Equipment needed: White paper (8.5x11), magic markers, blackboard, chalk

Directions:

(1) The teacher writes several (five to ten) characters (e.g., 本 , 未 , 末) or recently taught expressions on the blackboard. The length of each expression should not exceed three characters. The students copy down those words or expressions on their paper, one per page.

(2) The students form a circle and place their papers in front of them face down.

(3) The teacher says yī, èr, sān (一 , 二 , 三)! When the students hear the word sān 三 , they pick up one of the character sheets and hold it in front of them so everybody can see everybody else's words.

(4) If a student spots someone holding the same word as s/he has, s/he says the following as quickly as s/he can:

(The other student's name) yě yǒu (也有) (the word they are both holding).

47

If a student says this line before the other student does, s/he collects the sheet the other student is holding. If the other student says the line first, then s/he will have to give that other student his/her sheet.

(5) In the event that there are more than two persons holding the same word, one continues calling the names of all those who have the same word as the one one is holding. As long as one calls others' names before the others, they must give him/her their paper. Since the students will be screaming at each other, it will sometimes be hard to decide who has said the line first. Thus, it is important that the teacher serves as the referee and decides who the winners are. Also, the teacher must serve to decide whether a student has said both the other student's name and the common word correctly. In other words, in order to win other students' sheets, one needs not only to speak quickly but also correctly.

(6) After the winning students collect their sheets, or if no two students hold the same word, the teacher says "yī, èr, sān!" (一 , 二 , 三) again, and the students pick up a different sheet to display in front of them.

(7) The game ends when the designated time is up. The student who has collected the most sheets is the winner.

Identifying Characters

Skills addressed: Reading, Speaking
Suggested level of usage: Elementary or higher
Group size: Flexible
Equipment needed: Paper, magic markers

Directions:

(1) The teacher copies some recently taught characters on paper, one character per sheet.

(2) The teacher assigns one number to each of the students and writes them on paper, one number per sheet. The teacher divides the class into two teams--the odd-number team and the even-number team--and also separates the number sheets into two piles--the odd-number pile and the even-number pile.

(3) The teacher draws out one sheet from the character-sheet pile and shows the character--for example, xué 學 (study)--to the students. S/he also draws a number from the odd-number pile. The student whose number is drawn must swiftly identify the character xué 學 by saying (for example): xué, xuéshengde xué (學，學生的學).

(4) If the student identifies the character promptly and correctly, s/he gets two points. If s/he fails to identify it, her/his teammates can identify the character for her/him, with the team thereby receiving one point. The teacher then draws another character and a number from the even-number pile, and play rotates to the opposing team.

(5) If none of the students on the odd-number team recognizes the character, the teacher draws a number from the even-number pile, and the student whose number is drawn attempts to identify the character. If s/he is correct, s/he receives two points. If s/he fails, her/his teammates also have a second chance, but again they receive only one point if correct.

(6) The game ends when all the characters have been shown and identified, or when the predetermined time is up. The team with the most points is the winner.

6. WRITING VOCABULARY GAMES

Fill In the Missing Strokes

Skills addressed: Reading, Writing
Suggested level of usage: Elementary or higher
Group size: Flexible
Equipment needed: Paper, pens

Directions:
(1) The teacher prepares a handout with ten sentences written in Chinese characters. The sentences should include words the students are familiar with. Moreover, the sentences should include some characters with strokes missing. For example, the sentence 他不會寫字 might include "variants" 化, 會, or 字 for the first, third and fifth characters respectively.

(2) The teacher gives the handout to the students and allows them from five to ten minutes to spot and correct the flawed characters.

(3) After the time is up, the students can either read the sentences aloud or write the sentences (correctly) on the blackboard, in either case indicating the original mistakes.

(4) Students grade themselves, with one point given for each mistake spotted and properly corrected. The student with the highest point total is the winner.

Merry-Go-Round

Character component variation
Skills addressed: Writing, Reading
Suggested level of usage: Elementary or higher
Group size: 3-15
Equipment needed: Blackboard, chalk

Directions:
(1) The instructor picks any character the students have learned and writes it on the blackboard.

(2) The first student tries to "connect" with this character by using one component from it and writing the new character on the blackboard. For example, if the teacher has written the character huà　話, the student can use either yán 言 or shé 舌 to create a different character (e.g., yǔ 語 , huó 活). The character must be one the class has learned.

(3) If the student successfully "connects", s/he receives a point. If s/he does not, no point is awarded. Characters may not be repeated.

(4) Play continues to rotate until either a fixed point total or a time limit is reached. The player with the highest score is the winner.

(5) This game can also be played on a team basis, with play rotating between two or three teams. The team with the highest score at the end of the game is the winner.

53

Full character variation
Skills addressed: Writing, Reading
Suggested level of usage: Elementary or higher
Group size: 3-15
Equipment needed: Blackboard, chalk

Directions:
(1) The instructor picks any two-, three-, or four-character combination the students have learned and writes it on the blackboard.

(2) The first student uses one of the characters to form another polycharacter compound, writing that new combination on the blackboard. For instance, if the instructor has written <u>chīfàn</u>　吃　飯 on the board, the student may use either <u>chī</u> 吃 (e.g., <u>hǎochī</u> 好吃 , <u>chībuliǎo</u> 吃 不 了) or <u>fàn</u> 飯 (e.g., <u>fànguǎn</u> 飯 館 , <u>mǐfàn</u> 米 飯) in creating another expression. The maximum number of characters in each student's word or phrase should not exceed four.

(3) If the student successfully creates a compound, s/he receives a point. If s/he does not, no point is awarded. Expressions may not be repeated.

(4) Play continues to rotate until either a fixed point total or a time limit is reached. The player with the highest score is the winner.

(5) This game can also be played on a team basis, with play rotating between two or three teams. The team with the highest score at the end of the game is the winner.

Relay Race

Character formation variation
Skills addressed: Writing, Listening
Suggested level of usage: Elementary or higher
Group size: Flexible
Equipment needed: Blackboard, chalk

Directions:
(1) The teacher prepares in advance a list of Chinese characters the students have learned.

(2) The teacher divides the class into two teams and asks the students to form two lines several feet away from the blackboard.

(3) The teacher reads a character from the list, thereupon signaling that the game is on. Upon getting the signal, the first student on each team runs to the blackboard and writes down the first stroke of that character. S/he then rushes back to her/his line and hands the chalk to the next person in line. The next person then runs to the blackboard and writes down the second stroke of the character. The game continues until one of the two teams completes the character, with the winning team receiving one point.

(4) If a student writes a wrong stroke on the blackboard, the next student must erase the wrong stroke and write the correct one. That, of course, means that the team has wasted some time and might lose the round.

(5) Play continues until all the characters are read and written, or when the predetermined time is up. The team with the highest point total is the winner.

Sentence formation variation
    Skills addressed: Listening, Writing
 Suggested level of usage: Elementary or higher
      Group size: Flexible
   Equipment needed: Blackboard, chalk

Directions:

(1) The teacher prepares in advance a number of sentences using characters the students have learned.

(2) The teacher divides the class into two teams and asks the students to form two lines several feet away from the blackboard.

(3) The teacher reads a sentence from the list, thereupon signaling that the game is on. Upon getting the signal, the first student on each team runs to the blackboard and writes down the first character in the sentence. S/he then rushes back to her/his line and hands the chalk to the next person in line. The next person then runs to the blackboard and writes down the second character in the sentence. Play continues in a similar manner until one of the two teams completes the sentence, with the winning team receiving one point.

(4) If a student writes a character incorrectly, the next student must erase that character and rewrite it correctly.

(5) Play continues until all the sentences are read and written, or when the predetermined time is up. The team with the highest point total is the winner.

Group Dictation

Skills addressed: Listening, Reading, Writing
Suggested level of usage: Elementary or higher
Group size: Flexible
Equipment needed: Blackboard, colored chalk

Directions:

(1) Before the game, the teacher prepares a group of sentences that can be broken down into basic components such as subject, stative verb, adverb, object, etc. The teacher will also arbitrarily assign a color of chalk for each component.

(2) The teacher divides the class into as many teams as there are components to be considered. This can range from as few as two to as many as eight, depending on the class size and proficiency level.

(3) To start the game, the teacher reads one of the sentences aloud. One member from each team then goes to the blackboard and writes his/her team's assigned component (in Pīnyīn 拼音 or character form, depending on the students' level) from the sentence if such a component type appears in the sentence. For example, say there are four teams whose respective sentence components are subject, adverbial, stative verb, and particle. If the sentence read is Tā bú lèi le 他 不 累 了, all four team representatives would step up to the blackboard and write their part of the sentence. If, however, the sentence read is Tā hěn lèi 他 很 累, the "particle team" would not move.

58

Similarly, <u>Tā lèi le</u> 他 累 了 should elicit no response from the "adverbial team."

(4) One point is awarded for each correct component identification and one point subtracted for each incorrect one.

(5) Play continues until all the sentences have been read, or until a designated time limit. The team with the highest point total is the winner.

7. SEMANTIC VOCABULARY GAMES

The Definition Game

Skills addressed: Listening, Reading, Writing, Speaking
Suggested level of usage: Intermediate or higher
Group size: Flexible (minimum 3-5)
Equipment needed: Paper, pens

Directions:

(1) Before the game, the teacher prepares a list of five to ten words or phrases that the students have been learning. S/he writes each expression on a separate 8.5x11 sheet of paper.

(2) The teacher divides the class into several teams of three to five students.

(3) The teacher shows one of the words or phrases to the teams. They are thereupon allowed two minutes to determine the best possible definition (in Chinese) for that expression and to write that definition on a sheet of paper. The students may consult freely with their fellow team members.

(4) When the two minutes are up, the teacher asks a representative of each team to read his/her group's definition. The teacher then awards points based upon the

definition's grammatical and descriptive quality. Two points will be given for an outstanding definition, one point for an acceptable one, and no points for a (grammatically or semantically) incorrect definition.

(5) If a team disagrees with its opponent's definition for a given expression, it may challenge them, stating reasons (in Chinese, of course) for their disagreement. A team may also challenge the point total given either to themselves or to their opponents, again provided they supply compelling target-language argumentation. In all cases, the teacher shall be the final authority.

(6) Play continues until all the expressions have been shown and defined. The team with the highest point total is the winner.

Odd Word Out

Skills addressed: Reading, Writing, Listening, Speaking
Suggested level of usage: Elementary or higher
Group size: Flexible
Equipment needed: Paper, magic markers

Directions:

(1) The teacher divides the class into two teams and gives each team some paper and a magic marker.

(2) The teacher asks each team to prepare ten lists. Each list should contain five to seven words, all but one of which should belong to the same semantic category. Here are some examples:

chá, qìshuǐ, jiǔ, píjiǔ, **kāfēibēi**, Kěkǒukělè
茶, 汽水, 酒, 啤酒, 咖啡杯, 可口可樂

"Coffee cup" (**kāfēibēi** 咖啡杯) is the only thing on the list that is not a beverage.

xīngqīsān, lǐbàiliù, míngtiān, **wǔfēnzhōng,**
bādiǎnbàn, jiǔyuè
星期三, 禮拜六, 明天, 五分鐘, 八點半, 九月

"Five minutes" (**wǔfēnzhōng** 五 分 鐘) is a time-duration time word. All the rest are time-when time words.

chēpiào, chuánpiào, fēijīpiào, diànyǐngpiào, ménpiào, yóupiào

車票，船票，飛機票，電影票，門票，郵票

Everything on the list except "stamps" (yóupiào 郵票) are kinds of tickets.

(3) To play the game, team A shows a list to team B. Team B must determine the "odd" word, and also explain why that word does not belong to the group. The members of team B may consult with each other and let a representative respond on behalf of the team. If s/he points out the correct "odd" word with a satisfactory explanation, the team gets one point. It is then team B's turn to show team A one of the ten lists they prepared and ask team A to point out the "odd" word.

(4) The game ends when all the lists have been shown. The team with the highest point total wins.

What Kind of Noise Is It?

Skill addressed: Speaking
Suggested level of usage: Elementary or higher
Group size: Flexible
Equipment needed: Tape recorder, cassette tape

Directions:
(1) The teacher prepares a tape with various sounds on it (e.g., car, train, chalk writing on the blackboard, hands clapping, dog barking, etc.). Each sound should last ten to fifteen seconds.

(2) The teacher assigns one number to each of the students and divides the class into two teams--the odd-number team and the even-number team. The teacher also writes each number on a 3x5 index card and divides the cards into odd and even piles.

(3) The teacher plays one sound from the tape and then draws a card from the odd-number pile. The student whose number is drawn must quickly identify, in Chinese, what sound was just played. If s/he gives the correct answer, s/he earns two points for the team. If her/his answer is incorrect , or if s/he is unable to respond, her/his teammates may answer the question. If their answer is correct, the team will earn one point.

(4) If the odd-number team as a group is unable to identify the noise, the even-number team gets a chance to say what the sound was. The even-number team will receive two points if it identifies the noise correctly.

64

(5) Play rotates from team to team, one sound at a time. The game ends when all of the tape has been played, or when the predetermined time is up. The team with the highest point total is the winner.

8. BASIC SENTENCE GENERATION GAMES

Who Am I?

Skills addressed: Speaking, Listening
Suggested level of usage: Elementary
Group size: Flexible
Equipment needed: Student roster, scarf (or anything that can serve as a blindfold)

Directions:
(1) Several days before playing this game, the teacher prepares a roster of the students with their Chinese names transcribed into the romanization system the class uses. The teacher hands out the roster and asks the students to familiarize themselves with each other's Chinese names before the scheduled game day.

(2) The game itself begins as the teacher blindfolds a student and asks the rest of the students to take turns asking this question:

Wǒ shì shéi?
我是誰?

Upon hearing this question, the blindfolded student guesses who that student is by asking:

Nǐ shìbushì XXX (student's Chinese name)?
你是不是 XXX (student's Chinese name)?

If the blindfolded student guesses correctly, the student in question answers:

Duìle! Wǒ shì XXX (his/her Chinese name).
對了！我是 XXX (his/her Chinese name).

The blindfolded student then proceeds to guess the next student's name.

If, however, the guess is incorrect, the other student responds:

Búduì! Wǒ búshì XXX (the name guessed).
不對！我不是 XXX (the name guessed).

The blindfolded student then takes another guess. If his/her second guess is also incorrect, the student in question simply identifies himself/herself by saying:

Búduì! Wǒ yě búshì (the second name guessed), Wǒ shì XXX (his/her Chinese name).
不對！我也不是 (the second name guessed), 我是 XXX (his/her Chinese name).

(3) After the first student guesses all the names (or a predetermined number of names), another student is blindfolded and the game continues. The person who makes the fewest incorrect guesses is the winner.

Positive to Negative

Skills addressed: Listening, Speaking
Suggested level of usage: Elementary or higher
Group size: Flexible
Equipment needed: None

Directions:

(1) The teacher divides the students into two groups.

(2) The first student of team A starts the game by saying an affirmative sentence (e.g., <u>Wǒ yǒu qián</u> 我有錢).

(3) The first student of team B must negate the sentence within three seconds. If s/he responds with a correct sentence (e.g., <u>Wǒ méiyǒu qián</u> 我沒有錢), s/he then must also say an affirmative sentence of her/his choice, which the next person on team A must negate. If s/he fails to respond within three seconds or gives an incorrect sentence (e.g., <u>Wǒ bù yǒu qián</u> 我不有錢), team A loses one point and the turn goes to team B.

(4) A sentence may not be repeated. Violation of this will result in the team's losing one point and its turn.

(5) The game ends when the designated time is up. The team with the highest point total is the winner.

(6) Following are some of the more challenging positive-negative sentences:

a. <u>Tā lèile.</u> (He is tired)
他累了。

Correct: <u>Tā bú lèi</u>.
他不累。

Incorrect: <u>Tā méi lèi</u>.
他沒累。

b. <u>Tā láile</u>. (He has come)
他來了。

Correct: <u>Tā méi lái</u>.
他沒來。

Incorrect: <u>Tā bù láile</u>.
他不來了。

c. <u>Wǒ gēn tā qù</u>. (I go with her)
我跟她去。

Correct: <u>Wǒ bù gēn tā qù</u>.
我不跟她去。

Incorrect: <u>Wǒ gēn tā bú qù</u>.
我跟她不去。

d. <u>Tā duì Zhōngguó huà yǒu xìngqu</u>. (He is interested
in Chinese painting)
他對中國畫有興趣。

Correct: <u>Tā duì Zhōngguó huà méiyǒu xìngqu</u>.
他對中國畫沒有興趣。

Incorrect: <u>Tā búduì Zhōngguó huà yǒu xìngqu</u>.
他不對中國畫有興趣。

e. <u>Wǒ tīngdedǒng nǐ shuōde huà.</u>
我聽得懂你說的話。

Correct: <u>Wǒ tīngbudǒng nǐ shuōde huà.</u>
我聽不懂你說的話。

Incorrect: <u>Wǒ bù tīngdedǒng nǐ shuōde huà.</u>
我不聽得懂你說的話。

Restoring Sentences

Skills addressed: Reading, Writing, Speaking
Suggested level of usage: Elementary or higher
Group size: Flexible
Equipment needed: Paper, pens, 5x8 index cards

Directions:
(1) The teacher prepares ten sentences, breaking them down into their grammatical components, and writing each component on a separate 5x8 card. The sentences may be as simple as:

他　很　高。
1-1　1-2　1-3

or as complex as:

他　妹妹　的　朋友　吃飯　吃　得　很　快。
2-1　2-2　2-3　2-4　2-5　2-6　2-7　2-8　2-9

The numerical designators (Example:　2-1 stands for sentence 2, component 1) are suggested as means by which the teacher may mark the back of the 5x8 cards and ensure that his/her memory of the original sentence is retained.

For the most elementary students, Pīnyīn may be used instead of characters.

(2) One sentence at a time, the teacher places the component cards face up in nonsequential order. The cards

71

should be placed on a tabletop, or secured to the blackboard with magnets or tape, so that all students may clearly see them.

(3) The students are then instructed to "restore" the sentences from the components. Each student writes down his/her reconstruction on his/her own sheet of paper.

(4) After all the sentences have been shown and "restored," the teacher asks individual students to read aloud their reconstructed version. Other students as well as the teacher provide comments and corrections.

(5) Students grade themselves, with one point given for each correct sentence. The student with the highest point total is the winner.

What Could the Question Be?

Skills addressed: Writing, Reading, Listening,
Speaking
Suggested level of usage: Elementary or higher
Group size: Flexible
Equipment needed: Handouts (explained below),
pens

Directions:
(1) The teacher devises a two-person dialogue in Chinese
(either Pīnyīn or characters) in which speaker A asks ten
questions and speaker B gives ten answers to those
questions. The teacher then prepares a handout on which
only speaker B's answers appear.

(2) The teacher distributes the handouts and gives the
students from five to ten minutes to "create" a dialogue
based on the answers given.

(3) The teacher can either grade the student-devised
dialogues outside of class or have several students read
their dialogues aloud, with the whole class correcting and
commenting on the questions.

(4) The student who prepares the best dialogue is the
winner.

9. GRAMMATICAL PATTERN GAMES

Which Comes First?

Skills addressed: Listening, Speaking
Suggested level of usage: Elementary or higher
Group size: Flexible
Equipment needed: Blackboard, chalk

Directions:
(1) The teacher divides the class into two teams, and writes the following two sentence patterns on the blackboard:

A <u>yǐqián</u> B.

A <u>yǐhòu</u> B.

(2) The first student of team A (student A) starts the game by saying a sentence using one of the sentence patterns on the blackboard. For example:

<u>Tā chīfàn yǐqián xǐshǒu</u>.
他吃飯以前洗手。

or

74

Grammatical Pattern Games

Wǒ kànshū yǐhòu xiěxìn.
我看書以後寫信。

(3) The first student of team B (student B) is to decide which action takes place first and which action takes place next within three seconds. S/he then restates the sentence by using the following pattern:

Xiān A zài B, or xiān A hòu B.
先 A 再 B, or 先 A 後 B。

Therefore, when hearing sentence 1 above, student B's response should be:

Tā xiān xǐshǒu, zài (or hòu) chīfàn.
他先洗手, 再 (後) 吃飯。

When hearing sentence 2 above, student B's response should be:

Nǐ xiān kànshū, zài (or hòu) xiěxìn.
你先看書, 再 (後) 寫信。

(4) If student B responds correctly within the three-second limit, s/he then says a new sentence for the next person of team A (student C) to respond to. If student B fails to respond within three seconds, or if s/he mixes up the order of the actions, his/her team loses one point and its turn. Student C (on team A) will then continue the game by coming up with a new sentence.

75

(5) The same sentence may not be used twice. Violation of the rule will cause the team to lose its turn.

(6) The game continues until a designated time limit. The team with the highest score is the winner.

Scrambled Sentences

Skills addressed: Listening, Reading, Writing
Suggested level of usage: Elementary
Group size: Flexible
Equipment needed: 8.5x11 papers, pens

Directions:
(1) Each student folds an 8.5x11 sheet into six strips, tears off the strips, and numbers them 1 through 6. The students are then instructed to place the following informational components on the strips:

A. Subject of sentence (e.g., <u>Xiǎo Lǐ de gēge</u> 小李的哥哥)

B. Time-when phrase (e.g., <u>shàng xīngqīwǔ</u> 上星期五)

C. Origin (e.g., <u>cóng xuéxiào</u> 從學校)

D. Conveyance (e.g., <u>qí zìxíngchē</u> 騎自行車)

E. Destination (e.g., <u>dào shūdiàn qù</u> 到書店去)

F. Purpose (e.g., <u>mǎile yìběn zìdiǎn.</u> 買了一本字典)

(2) Six students will each gather all of one component (that is, all of the A's, all of the B's, etc.) and stand in alphabetical order (left to right, A through F) at the front of the classroom.

(3) Moving down the line, the students will draw at random from their strips and create new sentences (presumably at least occasionally of an amusing nature) by reading the components in sequence.

(4) While the students' laughter should confirm their comprehension, the teacher may wish to ask questions about the scrambled sentences to make sure that everyone gets the meaning.

Similarities and Dissimilarities

Skill addressed: Speaking
Suggested level of usage: Elementary or higher
Group size: Flexible
Equipment needed: Paper, pens, blackboard, chalk

Directions:
(1) The teacher prepares two pictures with many similarities but also with some dissimilarities. For example, the teacher may draw two boys differing in weight but not height, wearing clothes of the same style but different colors, etc. If the teacher has no time to prepare such pictures, s/he may use objects of such similarity/dissimilarity within the classroom.

(2) The teacher might also wish to write sentence patterns s/he wishes her/his students to use on the blackboard. For example:

A bǐ (比) B SV (stative verb).
Xiǎo Wáng bǐ Lǎo Lǐ ǎi. 小王比老李矮。

A bù bǐ (不比) B SV.
Xiǎo Wáng bùbǐ Lǎo Zhāng gāo. 小王不比老張高。

A méiyǒu (沒有) B nàme (那麼) SV.
Lǎo Zhāng méiyǒu Lǎo Lǐ nàme gāo.
老張沒有老李那麼高。

A gēn (跟) B yíyàng (一樣).
Zhèiběn shū gēn nèiběn shū yíyàng.
這本書跟那本書一樣。

79

A gēn (跟) B bù yíyàng (不一樣).
Yuánzǐbǐ gēn gāngbǐ bù yíyàng.
原子筆跟鋼筆不一樣。

A gēn (跟) B yíyàng (一樣) SV.
Màozi gēn shǒutào yíyàng guì.
帽子跟手套一樣貴。

A gēn (跟) B bù yíyàng (不一樣) SV.
Zhuōzi gēn yǐzi bù yíyàng dà.
桌子跟椅子不一樣大。

A de (的) X gēn (跟) B de (的) X yíyàng (一樣) SV.
Tāde biǎo gēn nǐde biǎo yíyàng guì.
他的錶跟你的錶一樣貴。

(3) The teacher divides the class into two groups. One team is assigned to name all the similarities in the pictures (or objects), and one all the dissimilarities.

(4) The team that is to point out the similarities plays first. Each team member takes a turn, naming one similarity at a time. If a member cannot point out a similarity, play goes to the other team, which will gain one point for each new similarity they point out.

(5) Play continues in a similar manner for the "dissimilarities team," which continues to name dissimilarities as long as their team members can identify them. If a member cannot, play goes to the "similarity team," which will gain one point for each unnamed dissimilarity they point out.

(6) Play continues until all the similarities and dissimilarities have been named, or until the students can

find no more. The team with the most points is the winner.

Specified sentence pattern variation
Skill addressed: Speaking
Suggested level of usage: Elementary or higher
Group size: Flexible
Equipment needed: Paper, pens, blackboard, chalk

Directions:

(1) The teacher prepares two pictures on separate sheets with many similarities but also with some dissimilarities. For example, the teacher draws two boys. One boy is tall and thin, and the other one is short and fat. Although they wear the same style of hat, one hat is blue and the other is red. They both wear yellow shirts, but one has two pockets and the other has only one pocket. Should the teacher have no time to prepare pictures, s/he can simply use two equally like/unlike objects from within the classroom.

(2) The teacher also writes down on the blackboard the sentence patterns s/he wishes his/her students to use. For example:

A bǐ (比) B SV (stative verb).
A bù bǐ (不比) B SV.
A méiyǒu (沒有) B nàme (那麼) SV.
A gēn (跟) B yíyàng (一樣).
A gēn (跟) B bù yíyàng (不一樣).
A gēn (跟) B yíyàng (一樣) SV.
A gēn (跟) B bù yíyàng (不一樣) SV.

81

A <u>de</u> (的) X <u>gēn</u> (跟) B <u>de</u> (的) X <u>yíyàng</u> (一樣) SV.

(3) The teacher divides the class into two groups. One team is assigned to name all the similarities in the pictures (or objects), and one all the dissimilarities.

(4) The teacher asks each member of the two teams to use one of the sentence patterns on the blackboard to point out one similarity or dissimilarity at a time. After the first member of team A says his/her sentence, the turn goes to the first member of team B, and then comes back to the second member of team A, etc. Each time a student fails to use the assigned pattern to form a sentence, s/he will lose one point and the turn goes to the other team.

(5) The game ends when the specified time is up or when the students have run out of identifiable similarities/ dissimilarities. The team with the highest point total is the winner.

The Linking Game

Skills addressed: Listening, Speaking
Suggested level of usage: Elementary or higher
Group size: Flexible
Equipment needed: 3x5 cards, pen

Directions:

(1) Before the game, the teacher prepares a list of five to ten pairs of subordinate sentence connective adverbs (e.g., yīnwei...suǒyǐ... [因爲...所以...] ; suīrán... kěshì... [雖然... 可是...]).

(2) The teacher divides the class into "odd" and "even" teams, with each student assigned a number, and each number written on a separate 3x5 card.

(3) The teacher draws a number from the "odd" stack; the student who has been assigned that number starts the game. The teacher then gives that student the first half of a subordinate sentence connective adverb pair (for example, yīnwei 因爲, or suīrán 雖然). The student must thereupon make up the first half of a sentence using that word.

(4) The teacher now draws an even-numbered card. The student whose number is drawn must complete the sentence (for the above examples, using suǒyǐ 所 以 or kěshì 可是).

(5) The next sentence would begin with the even-numbered team, with the odd-numbered team completing

the sentence. Play continues to rotate back and forth between the two teams in this manner.

(6) Two points are awarded each time a team member whose number is drawn completes his/her half of the sentence. If s/he cannot do so, his/her teammates may do so for him/her, but only one point is awarded if they do so correctly.

(7) Play continues until all the sentence constructions have been used. The team with the highest point total is the winner.

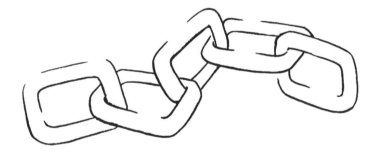

10. TIMEWORD-ORIENTED GAMES

What Time Is It?

Skill addressed: Speaking
Suggested level of usage: Elementary
Group size: Flexible
Equipment needed: Blackboard and chalk or
clock(s)

Directions:

(1) The teacher draws a clock on the blackboard or puts a clock in front of the class. The game will move faster if the teacher draws (or brings) two clocks.

(2) The teacher divides the class into two team and asks the students to line up standing in front of the clock(s).

(3) The teacher starts the game by "setting" the clock to any time and asking the first student of team A (student A) "Xiànzài jǐdiǎn zhōng (現 在 幾 點 鐘)?" or "Xiànzài shì shénme shíhou (現 在 什 麼 時 候)?" If student A answers the question promptly and correctly, s/he may set the clock to a new time and asks the same question of the first student on team B (student B).

(4) If student A fails to answer the teacher's question correctly, team A loses one point, and student B gets to answer the question.

(5) To make students practice kè 刻 (as in wǔdiǎn sānkè 五點三刻), bàn 半 (as in shíerdiǎn bàn 十二點半), and chà 差 (as in sìdiǎn chà wǔfēn 四點差五分), it is recommended that the students use kè 刻 and bàn 半 whenever they can and that they use chà 差 when it is less than fifteen minutes before an hour.

(6) The game continues until a designated time limit. The team with the highest score is the winner.

What Date Is It?

Skills addressed: Listening, Speaking
Suggested level of usage: Elementary
Group size: Flexible
Equipment needed: None

Directions:

(1) The teacher divides the class into two teams.

(2) The teacher starts the game by asking a date-oriented question. For example:

Jīntiān shì xīngqīliù, hòutiān shì xīngqījǐ?
今天是星期六，後天是星期幾？

The first student of team A must answer:

Hòutiān shì xīngqīyī.
後天是星期一。

S/he then goes on to ask the first student of team B a similar question. For example:

Xiàgeyuè shì yíyuè, xiànzài shì jǐyuè?
下個月是一月，現在是幾月？

(3) If the student answers the question correctly, her/his team receives two points. If the student fails to respond promptly, or if s/he responds incorrectly, one of her/his

teammates can jump in and give the correct answer. When this happens, the team receives one point.

(4) The game ends when the designated time is up. The team with the highest score wins.

(5) To keep all the students on their toes during the game, the teacher can assign a number to each of the players-- odd numbers for one team and even numbers for the other team. The teacher then writes the numbers on 3x5 index cards, one number on each card, and separates them into two piles, of odd and even numbers. Instead of letting the students take turns in sequence, the teacher draws out one number at a time from the two piles. When a student's number is drawn by the teacher, it is his/her turn to play.

Living Calendar

Skills addressed: Listening, Speaking
Suggested level of usage: Elementary
Group size: Flexible
Equipment needed: None

Directions:

(1) The teacher divides the class into two teams.

(2) The teacher starts the game by giving a date. For example:

<u>Wǔyuè bāhào xīngqīsì</u>
五月八號星期四

The first student of team A then says the next date and day of week. For example:

<u>Wǔyuè jiǔhào, xīngqīwǔ</u>
五月九號星期五

The first student of team B must then continue the sequence. For example:

<u>Wǔyuè shíhào, xīngqīliù</u>
五月十號星期六

(3) Play continues to rotate from team to team. Each time a student says the date correctly on her/his first try, the team receives two points. If the student fails to respond

89

promptly or if s/he makes a mistake, any of her/his teammates can jump in and help her/him out. If that response is correct, the team receives one point.

(4) The game ends when the designated time is up. The team with the highest point total is the winner.

(5) To keep all of the students on their toes during the game, the teacher can assign a number to each of the players--odd numbers for one team and even numbers for the other team. The teacher then writes the numbers on 3x5 index cards, one number on each card, and separates them into two piles, of odd and even numbers. Instead of letting the students take turns in sequence, the teacher draws out one number at a time from the two piles. When a student's number is drawn by the teacher, it is his/her turn to play.

11. QUESTION-ASKING PRACTICE GAMES

Get More Information

Skills addressed: Listening, Speaking
Suggested level of usage: Elementary or higher
Group size: Flexible
Equipment needed: None

Directions:
(1) The teacher makes a very general statement about some activity s/he has performed--e.g., <u>Zuótiān wǒ mǎile yìběn shū</u> (昨天我買了一本書).

(2) The students thereupon ask questions whereby they can gain more specific information about the action mentioned. For the example above, questions might include:

<u>Nèiběn shū shì zài nǎr mǎide?</u>
那本書是在那兒買的?

<u>Nǐ mǎide nèiběnshū yào duōshǎo qián?</u>
你買的那本書要多少錢?

(3) Students receive one point for each relevant and grammatically correct question. The student with the highest point total at the end of a predetermined time period is the winner.

Locating Your Friend

Skills addressed: Speaking, Listening, Writing
Suggested level of usage: Elementary or higher
Group size: Flexible
Equipment needed: Questionnaires (explained below)

Directions:
(1) Several days before playing the game, the teacher hands out questionnaires to the students. The questions may vary according to the students' proficiency, ranging from basic birth and family information to personal tastes and abilities. The questions may be in English, Pīnyīn, or character form.

(2) On the day before the game, the students turn in one copy of the questionnaire, keeping one copy for his/her own reference. The teacher then copies over each form in his/her own handwriting, omitting the students' names. This assures that a student will not recognize a classmate's handwriting.

(3) On the day of the game, the teacher hands out one sheet to each student, making sure that a student does not receive his/her own questionnaire. The students then move around the classroom asking questions based upon the information contained in the questionnaire in an attempt to match their sheet with the student it describes. Students may ask questions in any grammatically correct form, so long as they do not directly ask something like Zhèi (pointing at sheet) shì nǐ xiěde ma (這是你寫的嗎)?

(4) The students continue to ask questions until a "match" is made. The first student to correctly match the sheet and its author is the winner.

(5) For classes in which the students are well acquainted with each other's backgrounds, it might prove both more effective and interesting to encourage the students to create fictitious information about themselves. As long as they understand that they must stick to their questionnaire-generated "biography," the game is still quite playable.

12. RECONSTRUCTION/ DRAWING GAMES

The Artist Game

Skill addressed: Listening
Suggested level of usage: Elementary or higher
Group size: Flexible (small group to large class)
Equipment needed: Paper and pencil

Directions:
(1) Before the game, the teacher draws a simple picture containing objects whose Chinese names the students have learned.

(2) To play the game, the teacher first asks each student to take out a piece of paper and a pencil. The teacher then looks at the picture s/he has prepared and starts to describe the content of the picture in Chinese. The students must draw what they hear. For example:

If the picture prepared by the teacher looks like this,

zuǒ   yòu

左   右

the teacher can say:

Qǐng huà yìzhāng zhuōzi gēn yìbǎ yǐzi.
請畫一張桌子跟一把椅子。

Zhuōzi zài yǐzide zuǒbian.
桌子在椅子的左邊。

Zhuōzishàng yǒu yìběn shū gēn yìzhī qiānbǐ.
桌子上有一本書跟一枝鉛筆。

Shū zài zhuōzide zhōngjiān, qiānbǐ zài shūde yòubian.
書在桌子的中間，鉛筆在書的右邊。

Yǐzi dǐxia yǒu yìshuāng xiézi.
椅子底下有一雙鞋子。

(3) The teacher then collects the drawings to see if the students have drawn anything incorrectly. The student whose picture most closely resembles that of the teacher is the winner.

Copying the Picture

Skills addressed: Speaking, Listening
Suggested level of usage: Elementary or higher
Group size: Flexible
Equipment needed: Blackboard and chalk

Directions:
(1) The teacher prepares several pictures. The pictures can be fairly simple or rather complicated, depending on the level of the class. The important thing is that the things drawn on the pictures should be within the students' vocabulary, especially things the students have learned recently.

(2) The teacher divides the class into two teams. Each team elects an artist to go to the blackboard and stand in front of the blackboard with his/her back to the class.

(3) The teacher, standing between the two artists and the class, holds up a picture. S/he then asks the members of the two teams to take turns describing to their artist what they see, so that the artists can try to copy the picture on the blackboard. While the artists are drawing on the blackboard, the members of each team should point out mistakes their artist is making and ask him/her to improve the drawing. For example, if the artist is sketching a human figure, the team members might say:

Yǎnjing tài xiǎole, huà dà yìdiǎr!
眼睛太小了，畫大一點兒!

96

<u>Tāde zuǒshǒu dàizhe yìzhī shǒubiǎo, búshì yòushǒu!</u>
他的左手戴着一隻手錶，不是右手!

(4) The game ends when the predetermined time is up. The team that collectively produced the picture most closely resembling the teacher's original drawing is the winning team.

(5) Should the teacher decide to let the students practice their inventory of color words, colored chalk can be used.

(6) The teacher should remember that this is a language game, not a drawing contest. Accuracy is more important than artistry.

The Blind Artist

Skills addressed: Listening, Speaking
Suggested level of usage: Intermediate or higher
Group size: 2-5
Equipment needed: Blackboard, chalk, eraser

Directions:

(1) The teacher divides the class into several groups. Each group selects an artist, who is then blindfolded.

(2) The teacher draws a simple picture (e.g., a face, a house, etc.) on the blackboard. The artists attempt to copy it by following the instructions given by their teammates.

(3) The teammates take turns giving directions to their team artist. As might be expected, the picture drawn by the blindfolded artist can easily be too small or too big. If the drawing is a face, the eyes and the nose can be situated in the wrong position. It is the duty of the teammates to help their artist correct his/her mistakes by giving detailed directions. Some frequently used directions are:

Yǎnjing huà dà yìdiǎr!
眼睛畫大一點兒!

Bízi huàde tài gāole, bǎ tā cāle, chóng huà.
鼻子畫得太高了,把它擦了, 重畫!

(4) Each team is only allowed a fixed amount of time. When its time is up, the turn goes to the next team whether the picture is completed or not.

(5) At the end of the game, the team that has produced the picture most closely resembling the teacher's original is the winner.

13. RECOLLECTION GAMES

Can You Remember the Picture?

Location variation
> *Skills addressed*: Listening, Writing
> *Suggested level of usage*: Elementary or higher
> *Group size*: Flexible
> *Equipment needed*: Blackboard, chalk, paper, pens

Directions:

(1) The teacher draws a picture of a street scene with various business establishments and objects on the blackboard or on a piece of paper. The teacher allows the students thirty seconds to look at the picture before s/he covers or erases it.

(2) The teacher then asks the students to prepare pen and paper and to answer questions based on the picture. Questions might include:

> Jiàotáng zài nǎr?
> 教堂在哪兒?
>
> Lùshang yǒu jǐge rén?
> 路上有幾個人?
>
> Shūdiànde yòubian yǒu shénme?
> 書店的右邊有什麼?

Qìchē shìbushì zài fànguǎnde qiántou?
汽車是不是在飯館的前頭?

(3) The answers should be written in Chinese, either romanized or characters, depending on the students' proficiency. The person who makes the fewest mistakes is the winner.

(4) To make this game easier, the teacher may leave the picture on the blackboard instead of erasing it.

Comparison variation
            Skills addressed: Listening, Writing
Suggested level of usage: Elementary or higher
            Group size: Flexible
    Equipment needed: Blackboard, chalk, paper, pens

Directions:
(1) The teacher draws a picture on the blackboard or on a piece of paper. The picture must contain two or more objects the students can compare with each other (e.g., a tall skinny man and a short fat woman). After showing the picture to the students for thirty seconds, the teacher covers or erases the picture.

(2) The teacher then asks the students to prepare pen and paper and answer questions. Questions might include:

Nèige nánde bǐ nèige nǚde pàng ma?
那個男的比那個女的胖嗎?

Nèige nánrén gēn nèige nǚrén yíyàng gāo ma?
那個男人跟那個女人一樣高嗎

Nèige nǚde yǒu nèige nánde nàme gāo ma?
那個女的有那個男的那麼高嗎?

(3) The answers should be written in Chinese, either romanized or characters, depending on the students' proficiency. The person who makes the fewest mistakes is the winner.

(4) To make this game easier, the teacher may leave the picture on the blackboard instead of erasing it.

Can You Memorize the Objects?

Skills addressed: Listening, Speaking
Suggested level of usage: Elementary or higher
Group size: Flexible
Equipment needed: Objects (e.g., hat, scarf, gloves, shoes, coffee cup, wine bottle, etc.), or pictures of objects

Directions:

(1) The teacher prepares twenty to thirty objects (or pictures of those objects) for the game.

(2) The teacher divides the class into teams, with 3-5 students on each team.

(3) The teacher shows five to ten objects (or pictures) at a time, for a period of thirty seconds. S/he then puts the objects (or pictures) out of sight.

(4) The teacher then asks these questions:

Gāngcái nǐmen kànjiànle něixie dōngxi?
剛才你們看見了哪些東西?

Qǐng gàosu wǒ nèixie dōngxide míngzi!
請告訴我那些東西的名字!

(5) The members of each group then pool their memories and compile a list. As soon as a team thinks that it collectively remembers all the objects, the representative of that team should raise his/her hand to get the right to answer the question.

(6) The teacher then gives permission by saying:

<u>Qǐng nǐmen měigerén gàosu wǒ yíge míngzi</u>!
請你們每個人告訴我一個名字!

(7) The teammates take turns saying the names of the objects until they have named everything. Each time they say a name correctly, the team receives one point. For each mistake they make, the team loses **five** points.

(8) If one team fails to complete the list by giving the wrong name or forgetting something, other teams can take over and win (or lose) points.

(9) The teacher then displays a different set of objects on the desk and starts the second round of the game. The same objects (or pictures) may be used again.

(10) The game ends when the predetermined time is up. The team that has the highest point total is the winner.

14. BASIC DESCRIPTION AND NARRATIVE GAMES

Leading the Blind

Skills addressed: Listening, Speaking
Suggested level of usage: Elementary or higher
Group size: 2-5
Equipment needed: Empty space with objects that can be used as obstacles (e.g., classroom with movable chairs)

Directions:
(1) The teacher divides the class into several small groups. Each group selects a representative to play the "blind" person.

(2) The students arrange the furniture to make the room look like an obstacle course. If it is inconvenient to move the furniture around, the students may simply scatter some books and pens on the ground.

(3) The representatives are blindfolded and asked to go through the room by following the directions given by their team members. The team members are to help their representative go through the obstacle course safely (i.e., without running into or stepping on anything) in the shortest possible time. Typical directions are as follows:

Wàng qián zǒu sānbù!
往前走三步!

Wàng yòu zhuǎn!
往右轉!

Wàng zuǒ zhuǎn sìshíwǔdù, zài wàng qián zǒu yíbù!
往左轉四十五度，再往前走一步!

(4) When giving directions, all members of the team must participate so that everybody gets to practice giving directions.

(5) If a "blind" person steps on or runs into anything, s/he will be considered "dead," his/her team is out of the game, and the next team starts to play.

(6) The teacher keeps track of how much time each "blind" team member takes to go through the course. The team whose representive does it safely in the shortest time is the winner.

The Big Wind Blows

Skills addressed: Listening, Speaking
Suggested level of usage: Elementary or higher
Group size: Flexible
Equipment needed: None

Directions:

(1) The students gather their chairs in a circle. There should be one chair less than the total number of students playing the game.

(2) One student is selected to start the game as the guǐ 鬼 (ghost or "it"). The remaining students sit in the chairs while the guǐ stands in the middle.

(3) The student who is serving as guǐ starts the game with the following line:

Dà fēng chuī!
大風吹!

The remaining students respond by saying:

Chuī shénme?
吹什麼?

To this, the guǐ responds with any description that could apply to any or all of the students, preceded by the word chuī. Examples include:

107

<u>Chuī chuān hóng yīfude rén.</u>
吹穿紅衣服的人。

<u>Chuī dài yǎnjìngde rén.</u>
吹戴眼鏡的人。

<u>Chuī méi dài shǒubiǎode nán xuésheng.</u>
吹沒戴手錶的男學生。

<u>Chuī chuān lán kùzi gēn hēi píxiéde rén.</u>
吹穿藍褲子跟黑皮鞋的人。

(4) If a student recognizes him/herself as being a member of the "windblown" group, s/he must stand up and move to another seat. Simultaneously, the <u>guǐ</u> also attempts to take a chair. The student who is unable to find a seat becomes (or remains) the <u>guǐ</u>.

(5) If a student should have moved (i.e., if the <u>chuī</u> [description] expression described him/her) but did not, or should not have moved but did move, s/he must serve as the <u>guǐ</u> for the next turn.

(6) Play continues until a designated time limit.

The Association Game

Skills addressed: Listening, Speaking
Suggested level of usage: Intermediate or higher
Group size: Flexible
Equipment needed: 3x5 index cards

Directions:
(1) The teacher assigns one number to each student and divides the class into two teams--the odd-number team and the even-number team. The teacher writes each number down on 3x5 index cards and divides the cards into two piles--the odd-number pile and even-number pile.

(2) The teacher starts the game by giving a word of one or two characters (e.g., <u>màozi</u> 帽子, <u>biǎo</u> 錶, <u>píjiǔ</u> 啤酒, etc.).

(3) The teacher draws a card from the odd-number pile. The student whose number is drawn must quickly say a word related to that of the teacher, and also explain why the two words are related. For example, if the teacher says <u>biǎo</u> (watch), the student can say <u>zhōng</u> (clock) followed by this explanation:

<u>Biǎo gēn zhōng dōu kěyǐ ràng rén zhīdao shíjiān.</u>
錶跟鐘都可以讓人知道時間。

(4) If the student responds promptly and with a satisfactory explanation, s/he gets two points. If s/he is unable to respond, her/his teammates can answer for her/him, but they receive only one point for the correct

109

answer. No points are awarded for an unsatisfactory answer (in terms of either grammar or content).

(5) The turn then goes to the even-number team. The teacher draws a number from the even-number pile, and the student whose number is drawn must come up with a word related to the last word provided by the odd-number team.

(6) The game ends when the predetermined time is up. The team with the highest point total wins.

Make It Reasonable

Skills addressed: Listening, Reading, Writing,
Speaking
Suggested level of usage: Elementary or higher
Group size: Flexible
Equipment needed: Paper, pens

Directions:
(1) The teacher divides the class into two teams. Each
team is instructed to come up with ten sentences within
which there is some element of exaggeration (e.g., <u>Wǒ
chīle yíge liǎngchǐ chángde xīguā</u> [我吃了一個兩尺長的西
瓜]) or illogicalness (e.g., <u>Wǒ bǐ wǒ gēge dà sān suì</u> [我比
我哥哥大三歲]).

(2) Each team alternates in reading one sentence at a
time. The opposing team must make a correction in order
to earn a point. If the team whose sentence is being
corrected feels the correction is faulty, they may challenge
the correction. The teacher, as ever, serves as the final
authority.

(3) Play continues until all the sentences have been read,
or until a designated time limit. The team with the
highest point total is the winner.

111

15. ROLE-PLAYING GAMES

Who Is the Best Waiter/Waitress?

Skills addressed: Listening, Speaking, Writing
Suggested level of usage: Elementary or higher
Group size: Flexible
Equipment needed: Paper, pens, magic markers

Directions:
(1) The teacher prepares a menu of ten to twenty Chinese dishes. The menu can also include names of drinks. The teacher hands out the menu several days before the game and asks the students to study (or memorize) it. Additionally, the teacher may wish to provide dish-ordering vocabulary if the students have not yet learned it.

(2) On the day of the game, the teacher divides the class into groups of five students. One student in each group plays the waiter or waitress, and the rest play customers.

(3) One group at a time, the waiter/waitress takes orders from the other four members of the group. Typical questions by the waiter include:

Yàobuyào hējiǔ?
要不要喝酒？

112

Nín yào hē shénme jiǔ?
您要喝什麼酒？

Nín diǎn shénme cài?
您點什麼菜？

Nín yào jiào něige cài?
您要叫哪個菜？

Yàobuyào báifàn?
要不要白飯？

(4) As a customer, the player can order anything from the menu. S/he might even ask for things that are not on the menu but that all Chinese restaurants should have. For example:

Wǒ bù hē jiǔ, kěshì wǒ xiǎng hē chá. Qǐng nǐ gěi wǒ yìhú chá!
我不喝酒，可是我想喝茶。請你給我一壺茶！

Qǐng gěi wǒ yìshuāng kuàizi gēn yìwǎn báifàn!
請給我一雙筷子跟一碗白飯！

(5) After taking orders, the waiter/waitress goes to the "kitchen" to bring out the dishes and the food. While in real life a waiter/waitress usually writes down the orders, the waiter/waitress in this game is not allowed to use paper and pen. S/he must try to memorize all the orders. The "kitchen" is simply the teacher's desk with white paper and pens on it. The waiter/waitress writes down the names of the dishes and drinks on the paper, and "serves" the sheets to the customers.

113

(6) For each mistake the waiter/waitress makes, such as forgetting an order or serving the wrong dish, s/he loses one point.

(7) After all groups have been "served," the waiter or waitress who has made the fewest mistakes is judged the "best" waiter/waitress.

(8) After playing several times, the teacher might want to let all teams play simultaneouly to see which waiter/waitress can serve the most "dishes" to the most customers. Points are deducted for dishes either omitted or served to the wrong customers.

(9) If time allows, the teacher might also want to make the game longer by adding additional lines to it. For example, the waiter/waitress could add:

> Cài hái kěyǐ ba!
> 菜還可以吧!

and

> Yàobuyào lái diǎr tiándiǎn.
> 要不要來點兒甜點?

to which the customers could reply:

> Cài dōu hěn hǎo chī.
> 菜都很好吃。

and

> Búyào, chībuxiàle, qǐng bǎ zhàngdān nálai!
> 不要, 吃不下了, 請把帳單拿來!

114

Country Bumpkin

Skills addressed: Listening, Speaking
Suggested level of usage: Elementary or higher
Group size: Flexible
Equipment needed: None

Directions:
(1) One student is selected to play a newly arrived "country bumpkin" or "new kid in town." It is his/her task to find out as much as s/he can about the school and surrounding community from the other students. Questions as follows can be asked:

Qǐngwèn túshūguǎn zài nǎr?
請問圖書館在哪兒?

Zhèige xuéxiào yǒu duōshāo xuésheng?
這個學校有多少學生?

Wǒmen shénme shíhou fàngjià?
我們什麼時候放假?

Zhèige dōngxi jiào shénme? Nǐ kěyǐ bukěyǐ jiāo wǒ zěnme yòng?
這個東西叫什麼? 你可以不可以教我怎麼用?

Zhèrde dōngtiān cháng xiàxuě ma?
這兒的冬天常下雪嗎?

(2) Both the "bumpkin" and the other students receive one point for each relevant and grammatically correct question asked or answered. The student with the highest

point total at the end of the predetermined time period is the winner.

Confirming Relations

Skills addressed: Listening, Speaking
Suggested level of usage: Elementary or higher
Group size: Flexible
Equipment needed: None

Directions:
(1) The day before this game is to be played, students pair up under an assumed relationship (e.g., brothers/sisters, father/son, high school classmates). Prior to playing, they should get together to make sure they know all basic details about each other, such as: birthdate, age, birthplace, scholastic interests, likes and dislikes. These can be either genuine or fabricated details. The point is to make sure the partners "know" each other as well as real relatives or close friends. The preparation of a "fact sheet" on one's partner may prove useful, although this sheet should not be utilized during the actual game.

(2) On the day of the game, each pair in turn has one member (student A) leave the room while other students asks the member in the room (student B) about his/her partner's (student A's) history and traits in the aforementioned areas.

(3) The teacher awards points to both the questioners and student B on the basis of grammatical correctness and the quality of the questions and answers.

117

(4) Play continues until all the pairs have been questioned, or until a designated time limit. The pair with the highest point total is the winner.

(5) For classes in which the students are well acquainted with each other's backgrounds, it might prove both more effective and interesting to encourage the students to create fictitious information about themselves. As long as they understand that they must stick to their mutually understood stories, the game is still quite playable.

The Alibi Game

Skills addressed: Listening, Speaking
Suggested level of usage: Intermediate or higher
Group size: Flexible
Equipment needed: None

Directions:

(1) The day before this game is to be played, the teacher informs the class that a crime has been committed, and that everybody is a suspect. S/he asks the students to pair up and to work out their "alibi" prior to class the next day. This is, each student must be sure that s/he knows the whereabouts and activities of his/her partner throughout the day prior to the game.

(2) On the day of the game, each pair in turn has one member step outside while the other member is interrogated with questions such as

Nǐ zuótiān wǎnshang dào nǎr qùle?
你昨天晚上到哪兒去了?

Nǐ shì gēn shéi yíkuàr qùde?
你是跟誰一塊兒去的?

Nǐmen shì zěnme dào nàr qùde?
你們是怎麼到那兒去的?

Nǐmen dào nàr qù zuò shénme?
你們到那兒去做什麼?

Nǐmen shì jǐdiǎnzhōng huílaide?
你們是幾點鐘回來的?

119

(3) The teacher awards points to both the questioners and the questioned for grammatical correctness and pronunciation. If a pair fails to uphold each other's alibi, they are automatically eliminated from the game.

(4) Play continues until all the pairs have been questioned, or until a designated time limit. The team with the highest point total is the winner.

16. GROUP STORY GAMES

Group Story

Visual stimulus variation

Skills addressed:	Listening, Speaking
Suggested level of usage:	Elementary or higher
Group size:	Flexible
Equipment needed:	Ten to twelve photos or drawings of eveyday scenes, containing items that complement students' active vocabulary.

Directions:

(1) The teacher divides the class into two teams.

(2) The teacher shows one of the pictures and asks a member of the starting team to say something about it--up to three sentences, depending on the students' proficiency level. The student receives two points for an outstanding response, one point for an adequate one, and no points for a description that is flawed in terms of grammar or content. Students as well as the teacher should feel free to point out any errors.

(3) The teacher then shows another picture to a member of the second team. The student must not only provide an acceptable comment (syntactically and otherwise) on the

drawing or photograph, but must also draw some logical connection between the two pictures with his/her comment. For example, say the first drawing shown is that of a railroad station, prompting the first player to say:

Nà shì yíge huǒchēzhàn. Yǒu hěn duō rén zài nàr zuò huǒchē.
那是一個火車站。有很多人在那兒坐火車。

The second drawing of a restaurant can serve as an impetus for the next player to say:

Yīnwei tāmen zuò huǒchē zuòle hén jiǔ, suǒyǐ hěn è. Xià chē yǐhòu, yǒude rén jiù dào nèige fànguǎn qù chīfàn.
因爲他們坐火車坐了很久，所以很餓。下車以後，有的人就到那個飯館去吃飯。

Again, the teacher awards two, one, or zero points, with critical input from the students.

(4) Play continues until all the pictures have been shown, or until a designated time limit. The team with the highest point total is the winner.

(5) For advanced students, the teacher may prescribe that each student must retell the entire story up to the point at which s/he is called upon to continue it. Word-for-word repetition is not required, but the student must include all the critical details.

122

Oral variation
Skills addressed: Listening, Speaking
Suggested level of usage: Intermediate or higher
Group size: Flexible
Equipment needed: None

Directions:

(1) The teacher assigns a topic the students are familiar with and have learned enough vocabulary items to talk about.

(2) The students take turns saying sentences concerning the topic. Each student can say anything s/he wants, but the next student must say something that logically follows what was first said. In other words, a coherent story must be formed.

(3) It is the teacher's duty to point out and correct all mistakes the students make.

(4) If time allows, and as a means of further drill, the teacher may ask each student to repeat the story before s/he adds her/his line to it.

Written variation
Skills addressed: Reading, Writing
Suggested level of usage: Intermediate or higher
Group size: Flexible
Equipment needed: Blackboard, chalk

Directions:

(1) The teacher assigns a topic the students are familiar with and can write about in Chinese.

(2) The students form a line in front of the blackboard.

(3) Each student writes one sentence regarding or arising from the given topic. Each sentence added must logically follow what has already been written so a coherent story can take shape.

(3) It is the teacher's duty to point out all mistakes the students make.

17. INTERMEDIATE AN ADVANCED NARRATIVᴇ GAMES

Imitation

Skills addressed: Speaking, Listening
Suggested level of usage: Intermediate or higher
Group size: 3
Equipment needed: Various objects (within the students' vocabulary range)

Directions:

(1) The teacher assigns three roles to the three players. One will be the actor, one will be the imitator, and the other will be the director.

(2) The imitator sits or stands with his/her back to the actor.

(3) The actor starts to act or do things. For example, the actor can pretend that s/he is crying. The director is to describe in great detail what the actor is doing so that the imitator can perform an identical act. The director can give detailed descriptions such as:

<u>Tā yòng tāde zuǒshǒu cóng tāde kùzi kǒudàili náchūle
yìtiáo shǒupà.</u>
他用他的左手從他的褲子口袋裏拿出了一條手帕。

125

Tā yòng tāde yòushǒu bǎ tāde yǎnjìng zhāile xiàlai.
他用他的右手把他的眼鏡摘了下來。

Tā yòng shǒupà cā tāde yǎnlèi.
他用手帕擦他的眼淚。

(4) The director should point out the imitator's mistakes and help him/her to correct them by saying things such as:

Wǒ shuō tā yòng tāde yòushǒu, búshì tāde zuǒshǒu, bǎ tāde yǎnjìng zhāile xiàlai.
我說他用他的右手，不是他的左手，把他的眼鏡摘了下來。

Wǒ shuō cóng tāde kùzi kǒudàili, méi shuō cóng tāde shàngyī kǒudàili, náchūle yìtiáo shǒupà.
我說從他的褲子口袋裏，沒說從他的上衣口袋裏，拿出了一條手帕。

(5) Once the imitator has accurately performed, the teacher asks the students to switch roles so that all get to play the director. The teacher might also want to ask another student from the class to replace one of the players, thus rotating the students as often as possible.

126

Quick Story

Skills addressed: Speaking, Readin
Suggested level of usage: Advanced
Group size: Flexible
Equipment needed: Paper, pens

Directions:
(1) The teacher prepares in advance some topics (e.g., words the students have learned recently) and writes them down, one topic per sheet.

(2) The teacher assigns a number to each student and writes each number down on a separate sheet. The class is divided into two teams, the odd-number team and the even-number team.

(3) The teacher puts three piles of paper on the table: one pile for topics, one pile for odd numbers, and one pile for even numbers.

(4) The teacher draws a sheet from the topic pile, shows it to the students, and asks them to think of three sentences about the topic. After a few seconds, the teacher then draws a number from the odd-number pile. The student whose number is drawn must immediately say his/her three sentences. For each correct and meaningful sentence s/he says, the team earns two points. If that student says nothing, but other members of her/his team do have something to say, they can do so, with the team receiving one point for each correct sentence.

(5) The teacher then draws another topic and an even number, and the other team takes its turn to get some points.

(6) The game ends when all the expressions are used or when the predetermined time is up. The team with the most points is the winner.

18. CARD GAMES

Pulling the Blankets

Skills addressed: Listening, Speaking, Reading
Suggested level of usage: Elementary
Group size: 3-5

Equipment needed:
This game requires the use of either a standard deck of poker playing cards (Jack = 11, Queen = 12, and King = 13), or a specially constructed set of forty 3x5 index cards. The latter consists of four identical sets of ten cards with the Chinese characters 1 to 10 written on them, one number per card. You may increase the number of the sets if you wish. Also, if you want to let your students practice numbers up to 20 you can simply put 20 cards in each set to accommodate the numbers 1 to 20.

Directions:
(1) Each player is dealt an equal number of cards. The cards are to be stacked up in front of each player face down so that no one, including the player, is able to see what the cards are.

(2) Play may begin with any player, but whoever begins does so by saying yī 一 (one) as s/he picks up the top card from the pile of cards in front of her/him, turns it over and puts it in the middle of the table (or the game area). If the

card played happens to be an ace (ace stands for one in the standard deck), or the Chinese character y̲ī̲ — (if using the special deck), all the players must try to cover up the card with their hands, including the player who laid the card. The last person to do so is the loser and must pick up the card and lay it beside him/her.

(3) If the first card was not an ace or y̲ī̲ —, players continue to lay cards in a set direction and "count off" until such time as the number of the card played and called out coincide (e.g., a player says s̲h̲í̲ 十 while laying down a ten). As previously stated, the last player to put her/his hand over the card will be the loser. The loser must pick up all the cards played up to that point in the game. The more cards one takes, the bigger a loser one is.

(4) Every time a card played coincides with the number called there will be a loser who must pick up all card(s) played since the last coinciding card and number. After the cards are taken, the game resumes, starting from the person who is next to the player who played the last card. The numerical "counting off" process may continue from the last number called or begin from "one" once again.

(5) Play continues until all the cards have been laid. If the students complete the entire string of numbers (one through thirteen for those using the standard deck, one through ten or twenty for those using the special deck) without any number said and card played coinciding, they must start at one again, continuing until all the cards have been played.

(6) When all the cards have been played, or after a predetermined time limit, each player counts the cards s/he has taken. The person who has the fewest cards is the winner of that game.

Asking for Cards

Number variation
Skills addressed: Reading, Listening, Speaking
Suggested level of usage: Elementary
Group size: 3-5

Equipment needed:
This game requires the use of either a standard deck of poker playing cards (Jack = 11, Queen = 12, and King = 13), or a specially constructed set of forty 3x5 index cards. The latter consists of ten cards with the Chinese characters 1 to 10 written on them, one number per card. You may increase the number of the sets if you wish. Also, if you want to let your students practice numbers up to 20 you can simply put 20 cards in each set to accommodate the numbers 1 to 20.

Directions:
(1) Each player is dealt an equal number of cards, which s/he keeps hidden from her/his opponents. Before actual play begins, each player lays down all pairs of cards s/he has been dealt.

(2) Play may begin with any player. Whoever begins play asks any of her/his opponents for one card that will enable her/him to form a pair. The player must use Chinese. For example:

Qǐng wèn, nǐ yǒu mei yǒu (number desired)?
請問你有沒有 (number desired)?

(3) If the player questioned has no such card, s/he says <u>Duìbuqǐ, wǒ méiyǒu</u> 對 不 起 , 我 沒 有 (number desired), and play rotates to the next student.

(4) If the player questioned does have the card in question, the following dialog is carried out:

Questioned: <u>Wǒ yǒu</u> (number desired).
我有 (number desired).

Questioner: <u>Qǐng nǐ gěi wǒ yìzhāng</u> (number desired).
請你給我一張 (number desired).

Questioned: <u>Hǎo, wǒ gěi nǐ yìzhāng</u> (number desired).
好，我給你一張 (number desired).

Questioner: <u>Xièxie nǐ!</u>
謝謝你!

Questioned: <u>Búkèqi!</u>
不客氣!

(5) If the questioner gets a pair, s/he may continue to ask for cards. Play continues until one player has gotten rid of all of her/his cards in the form of pairs.

(6) It may be of value to ensure that students pay attention to pronunciation as a means of "protecting" their cards. Suppose a student asks: "<u>Qǐng wèn, nǐ yǒu mei yǒu jiù</u> 請 問 , 你 有 沒 有 '舊'?" (note tone on last word--the correct word for nine [九] is <u>jiǔ,</u> not <u>jiù</u>). Even if his opponent is holding a nine, that opponent is perfectly correct in replying, "<u>Duìbuqǐ, wǒ méiyǒu jiù</u> ("old") [對 不

133

起, 我 沒 有 舊]." This serves not only to heighten the competitive spirit, but also to impress upon the more careless students the need for accurate pronunciation.

(7) For the more advanced students, the game rules might be slightly modified so that the object is to collect as many pairs as possible rather than simply try to get rid of one's cards as quickly as possible.

Character variation
Skills addressed: Reading, Listening, Speaking
Suggested level of usage: Elementary
Group size: 3-5

Equipment needed:
Two sets of 3x5 cards, one character per card, covering at least a representative sampling (if not all) of the vocabulary the students have learned. The teacher might find it helpful to number a corner of each card with the lesson number in which the vocabulary item is introduced, so that s/he can add to or subtract from the set as necessary during the course of study. The cards must be of sufficient thickness, or the instrument with which the characters are written of a light enough color, so that the characters cannot be discerned through the back of the card when it is turned face down.

Directions:

(1) All players are dealt an equal number of cards, which they keep hidden from their opponents. Before actual play begins, each player lays down all pairs of cards s/he has been dealt.

(2) Play may begin with any player. Whoever begins play asks any of her/his opponents for one card that will enable her/him to form a pair. The player must use Chinese.

> Qǐng wèn, nǐ yǒu mei yǒu (character desired)?
> 請問你有沒有 (character desired)?

(3) If the player questioned has no such card, s/he says

> Duìbuqǐ, wǒ mei yǒu (character desired).
> 對不起，我沒有 (character desired).

and play rotates to the next student.

(4) If the player questioned does have the card in question, the following dialogue is carried out:

Questioned: Wǒ yǒu (character desired).
　　　　　　我有 (character desired).

Questioner: Qǐng nǐ gěi wǒ (character desired).
　　　　　　請你給我 (character desired).

Questioned: Hǎo, wǒ gěi nǐ (character desired).
　　　　　　好，我給你 (character desired).

Questioner: Xièxie nǐ!
　　　　　　謝謝你!

135

Questioned: <u>Búxiè</u>!
不謝!

(5) If the questioner gets a pair, s/he may continue to ask for cards. Play continues until one player has gotten rid of all of her/his cards in the form of pairs.

(6) It may be of value to ensure that students pay attention to pronunciation as a means of "protecting" their cards. Suppose a student asks: "<u>Qǐng wèn, nǐ yǒu mei yǒu</u> <u>**'hào'**</u>?" (note tone on last word--the intended word being "<u>hǎo</u>" 好 "good"). Even if his opponent is holding a "<u>hǎo</u>," that opponent is perfectly correct in replying, "<u>Duìbuqǐ,</u> <u>wǒ meiyǒu **'hào'**</u> [對不起，我沒有 '號']!" This serves not only to heighten the competitive spirit, but also to impress upon the more careless students the need for accurate pronunciation.

(7) If the questioner misreads a character (e.g., while asking for a "<u>nǐ</u>," 你 but saying <u>tā</u> 他 instead), s/he will get a card that is not the one s/he hoped to get in order to form a pair. When this happens, the questioner loses his/her turn.

(8) For the more advanced students, the game rules might be slightly modified so that the object is to collect as many pairs as possible rather than simply try to get rid of one's cards as quickly as possible.

136

Concentration

Character variation
Skills addressed: Reading, Speaking
Suggested level of usage: Elementary or higher
Group size: 3-7

Equipment needed:
Two sets of 3x5 cards, one character per card, covering at least a representative sampling (if not all) of the vocabulary the students have learned. The teacher might find it helpful to number a corner of each card with the lesson number in which the vocabulary item is introduced, so that s/he can add to or subtract from the set as necessary during the course of study. The cards must be of sufficient thickness, or the instrument with which the characters are written of a light enough color, so that the characters cannot be discerned through the back of the card when it is turned face down.

Directions:
(1) The teacher selects fifteen cards from one set and finds the fifteen that match them from another set. S/he then places them face down in a 5 by 6 card grid, making sure they do not appear in any special order. The teacher can, of course, increase the number of cards for more advanced students. However, to ensure that the game is manageable, no more than 60 cards should be used in any one game.

(2) The first student turns over one card, pronouncing the character s/he sees, and then repeats the process with a second card. If the student has found a matching pair and has pronounced the character correctly, s/he removes the pair and receives one point in her/his favor. If the two cards do not match, s/he turns them back over, and play rotates to the next student.

(3) Play continues until all the pairs have been removed. The player who accumulates the most points is the winner.

(4) While it is suggested that the character cards initially be set up in neat rows, one may lay out the cards in a more scrambled manner in order to increase the challenge as time goes on.

Pīnyīn Variation
Skills addressed: Reading, Speaking
Suggested level of usage: Elementary
Group size: 3-7

Equipment needed:
Fifteen to thirty pairs of 3x5 cards with Pīnyīn romanizations of various single-syllable Chinese words. The words do not have to be ones students have learned the meaning for, but should include ones that are consistent sources of confusion (e.g., the zhi/chi/shi, zi/ci/si and ji/qi/xi series).

Directions:

(1) The teacher places the cards face down on the tabletop, either in rows or a jumbled fashion, ensuring in either case that they do not appear in any predictable order.

(2) The first student turns over one card, pronouncing the character s/he sees, and then repeats the process with a second card. If the student has found a match (i.e., two identical syllables) and has pronounced them correctly, s/he removes the pair and receives one point. If the two cards do not match, s/he turns them back over, and play rotates to the next student.

(3) Play continues until all the pairs have been removed. The player with the highest point total is the winner.

Character/Pīnyīn variation
Skills addressed: Reading, Speaking
Suggested level of usage: Elementary or higher
Group size: 3-7

Equipment needed:
Two sets of 3x5 cards, preferably of two different colors (e.g., pink and yellow). One set of the cards is for characters, one character per card, and the other set is for the Pīnyīn equivalents of the characters. It is advised that the characters chosen for the cards be the ones the students have trouble pronouncing. The teacher might also find it helpful to number a corner of each card with

the lesson number in which the vocabulary item is introduced, so that s/he can add to or subtract from the set as necessary during the course of study. The cards must be of sufficient thickness, or the instrument with which the characters are written of a light enough color, so that the characters cannot be discerned through the back of the card when it is turned face down.

Directions:
(1) If the character cards and the Pinyin cards are of different colors, the teacher simply mixes the two sets of cards together and places the cards face down on the tabletop, either in rows or a jumbled fashion, ensuring in either case that they do not appear in any predictable order. If the character cards and the Pīnyīn cards are of the same color, the two sets should be separated so the students can tell whether a card is a character card or a Pīnyīn card.

(2) The first student turns over one card, pronouncing the character or Pīnyīn romanization s/he sees, and then repeats the process with a second card from the other set (which can be told by color or by location). If the student has found a match (i.e., a character and its Pīnyīn equivalent) and has pronounced both elements in the pair correctly, s/he removes them and receives one point. If the two cards do not match, s/he turns them back over, and play rotates to the next student.

(3) Play continues until all the pairs have been removed. The player with the highest point total is the winner.

Antonym variation
> *Skills addressed*: Reading, Speaking
> *Suggested level of usage*: Elementary or higher
> *Group size*: 3-7

Equipment needed:
One set of 3x5 cards, one character per card, covering at least a representative sampling (if not all) of the vocabulary the students have learned. The teacher might find it helpful to number a corner of each card with the lesson number in which the vocabulary item is introduced, so that s/he can add to or subtract from the set as necessary during the course of study. The cards must be of sufficient thickness, or the instrument with which the characters are written of a light enough color, so that the characters cannot be discerned through the back of the card when it is turned face down.

Directions:
(1) The teacher selects from the set of character cards five to fifteen pairs of antonyms (e.g., 大/小, 多/少), depending on the students' vocabulary level. S/he then places the cards face down, either in rows or a jumbled fashion, ensuring in either case that they do not appear in any predictable order.

(2) The first student turns over one card, pronouncing the character s/he sees, and then repeats the process with a second card. If the student has found a pair of antonyms and has pronounced the characters correctly, s/he removes the pair and receives one point. If the two cards do not

141

"match" (i.e., are not antonyms), s/he turns them back over, and play rotates to the next student.

(3) Play continues until all the pairs (of antonyms) have been removed. The player with the highest point total is the winner.

Connecting the Dragons

Skills addressed: Reading, Speaking
Suggested level of usage: Elementary
Group size: 3-7

Equipment needed:
Forty to eighty 3x5 index cards and four color pens (red, black, green, and blue). Divide the index cards equally into four sets, and write one Chinese number from 1 to 10 (or up to 20 depending on the number of cards in each set) on each of the cards in the four sets using the four different color pens. In other words, if there are forty cards, there should be four sets of 1 to 10 in four different colors. You may increase the number of sets if you wish to have more than four colors in the deck. This can easily be done by adding another 10 or 20 3x5 index cards to the deck with numbers 1 to 10 (or up to 20) written on them using a different color. However, to ensure that the game is easy to play and not too time-consuming, it is advised that you use no more than six colors and no more than 120 cards. The minimum requirement will be 40 cards and four colors.

Directions:
(1) All players are dealt an equal number of cards. The cards should be dealt face down, and players should keep their cards hidden from opponents' view.

(2) The player holding the middle number of a suit determined either by the teacher or the class commences

play by laying his/her card face up in the center of the table. For example, if each set has 13 cards and the predetermined color is red, Red 7 is laid first. If each set has 20 cards and the predetermined color is green, Green 10 is laid first. S/he must also say the number of that card in Chinese as s/he does.

(3) If the first player laid (for example) a Black 5, the next player has one of three choices, namely: (a) to lay a Black 6; (b) to lay a Black 4; (c) to lay a 5 of some other suit. Similarly, if, for example, play involves fifteen-card suits with the game-starting set determined to be blue, the initially laid Blue 8 may be followed by (a) a Blue 9, (b) a Blue 7, or (c) an 8 of some other suit.

(4) Play continues in a similar pattern. That is, one must either "follow suit," continuing the sequence either up or down in any of the suits showing, or start a new row of another suit (using the middle number). If the player can neither follow suit nor start a new row, s/he must discard one card into her/his pile. The discard should be low numerically, for reasons to be explained later.

(5) At the end of the game, the numbers on the cards discarded are added up. The higher the total, the bigger a loser one is. In other words, to win the game, one should try not to discard any cards, if possible. If one has to discard cards, one should discard lower number cards first--unless one wishes to "hurt" others. See explanations below.

(6) As the game progresses, a series of four "dragons" should begin to fill the table, as pictured below:

Black 7		Red 7	
Black 6	Green 6	Red 6	
Black 5	Green 5	Red 5	Blue 5
Black 4	Green 4		Blue 4
	Green 3		Blue 3
			Blue 2

(7) One element of strategy is to "hurt" other players by discarding a crucial card. Say a competitor facing the above playing situation has only three cards left, Black 2, Green 8, and Blue 7. S/he holds none of the cards with which s/he could continue the game (which would be Black 8, Black 3, Green 7, Green 2, Red 8, Red 4, Blue 6, and Blue 1). The player has to discard one of the three cards in her/his hand. Normally, Black 2 will be the right card to discard, because it is a low number. However, the player might want to discard Blue 7 to "hurt" his opponents. That is, since they are logically holding Blue 8, 9, and 10, s/he can effectively block any possibility of their finishing the game without discarding those high cards. Of course, they can practice similar strategy on him/her.

(8) Play continues until all participants have laid down their cards, either as part of the "dragons" or in their respective discard piles. The winner is the one who has managed to put all of his/her cards into dragons (a long shot), or the one who has the lowest point total in her/his discard pile.

Sentence Stringing

Skill addressed: Writing
Suggested level of usage: Elementary or higher
Group size: 3-5

Equipment needed:
This game can be played with either teacher-prepared sets of 3x5 index cards (one character per card), covering all characters learned by the student, or by using student-prepared flashcard sets. There are advantages to both approaches. The former ensures a uniformity of characters in terms of quality (with characters neatly and correctly written), although it forces the instructor to take the time to compile and keep "up to date" one set of cards for each student in the class. The latter provides a subtle impetus for the student to compile and continue to update his/her own set of learning aids, as those aids will also be of assistance in the competition described herein. We leave it to the teacher's discretion.

Directions:
(1) Each player is given (or provides) one set of character cards.

(2) The first player uses any one of her/his cards to start a sentence, pronouncing the word as s/he places it on the table.

(3) The object is simply to continue the sentence for as long as possible. If a student cannot add another character to

the sentence, s/he is assessed a penalty point and must start a new sentence.

(4) Play continues until a designated limit (time or points), at which time the player with the lowest score wins.

(5) The instructor's role must be continual to ensure not only that the sentences created are grammatically correct, but also that there is not repetition of the same sentences over and over again.

Pulling the Rickshaw

Skills addressed: Reading, Speaking
Suggested level of usage: Elementary or higher
Group size: 4-6

Equipment needed:
One set of 3x5 cards, one character per card, covering at least a representative sampling (if not all) of the vocabulary the students have learned. The teacher might find it helpful to number a corner of each card with the lesson number in which the vocabulary item is introduced, so that s/he can add to or subtract from the set as necessary during the course of study. The cards must be of sufficient thickness, or the instrument with which the characters are written of a light enough color, so that the characters cannot be discerned through the back of the card when it is turned face down.

Directions:
(1) All students are dealt an equal number of cards. There should be enough cards left over so there is a pile of reasonable size to draw from. One card is turned face up, serving as the start of the discard pile.

(2) The first player must lay a card that contains either the same initial, the same final, or the same radical as that showing on the discard pile. For example, if ní 你 is the first card showing, the next player could lay a nèi 那 (nèi has the same initial as ní), a xī 西 (xī has the same final as ní), or a tā 他 (tā has the same radical as ní). If the

player holds no such cards, s/he must draw a card from the draw pile, and continue to draw cards until s/he finds one that does match the initial, final, or radical of the card on the discard pile.

(3) Players must also pronounce each character card as they lay it down. If they fail to do so, or pronounce the character incorrectly, an extra card must be picked up from the draw pile.

(4) The first player to lay down all his/her cards is the winner.

SUBJECT INDEX

151

GAME INDEX